OLD LEATHER

AN ORAL HISTORY *of* EARLY PRO FOOTBALL *in* OHIO, 1920–1935

CHRIS WILLIS

THE SCARECROW PRESS, INC.
Lanham, Maryland • Toronto • Oxford
2005

796.332
W73σ

Cal

SCARECROW PRESS, INC.

Published in the United States of America
by Scarecrow Press, Inc.
A wholly owned subsidary of
The Rowman & Littlefield Publishing Group, Inc.
4501 Forbes Boulevard, Suite 200, Lanham, Maryland 20706
www.scarecrowpress.com

PO Box 317
Oxford
OX2 9RU, UK

British Library Cataloguing in Publication Information Available

Library of Congress Cataloging-in-Publication Data

Willis, Chris, 1970–
  Old leather : an oral history of early pro football in Ohio, 1920–1935 /
Chris Willis.
    p. cm.
  Includes bibliographical references and index.
  ISBN 0-8108-5660-3 (pbk. : alk. paper)
  1. Football—Ohio—History—20th century—Anecdotes. 2. National
Football League—History—20th century—Anecdotes. I. Title.

GV954.W55 2005
796.332'64'09771—dc22

                                                        2005002219

⊗™ The paper used in this publication meets the minimum requirements of
American National Standard for Information Sciences—Permanence of Paper
for Printed Library Materials, ANSI/NISO Z39.48-1992.
Manufactured in the United States of America.

Contents

Foreword   *Joe Horrigan*   v

Preface   vii

Acknowledgments   ix

Introduction   xi

 1   Lester H. Higgins   1

 2   Joseph F. Carr   5

 3   Fritz Pollard   12

 4   Nesser Brothers   18

 5   George "Hobby" Kinderdine   25

 6   Lee Fenner   28

 7   Ike Roy Martin   32

 8   Arda Bowser   36

 9   Art Haley   44

10   Walter Lingo   48

11   William Guthery, Sr.   53

12   William Roy "Link" Lyman   57

13   Hal Broda   62

14   Glenn Presnell   67

15   Dr. Louis Chaboudy   75

16   Leo Blackburn   81

17   Earl "Dutch" Clark   86

18   Cyrus Kahl   92

19   Norris Steverson   95

Overtime   99

Appendix: Complete Standings, Team Rosters,
Game Results, and Attendance Figures for all Ohio
Teams in the National Football League, 1920–1935   101

Notes   157

Index   169

About the Author   175

Foreword

B Y FAR, THE MOST FREQUENTLY ASKED QUESTION BY VISITORS TO THE
Pro Football Hall of Fame is "Why Canton?" And although there
is a colorful display near the museum's entrance detailing the answer, Hall of Fame staffers often share the Canton story before patrons
come upon the detailed storyboards.

The answer is neither simple nor short, but the Hall's frontline employees have related the tale enough times that they can pretty much get
to the heart of the matter before the querying customer loses interest.

The narrative usually starts like this: "The Pro Football Hall of Fame is
located in Canton, Ohio, for three primary reasons." And from there the
oft-told story is presented point by point. For the record, the three reasons
are as follows: First, the National Football League (NFL), originally known
as the American Professional Football Association, was founded in Canton
in 1920. Next, the Canton Bulldogs, a pro football power even before the
founding of the NFL, was the league's first two-time champion, capturing
titles in 1922 and 1923. And finally, but no less significantly, Jim Thorpe,
the game's first big-name performer and perhaps this country's greatest athlete, played several years for the Bulldogs beginning in 1915.

Although this local history lesson is usually new information for
Hall of Fame guests, that wasn't the case for Columbus, Ohio, native
and Hall of Fame visitor Chris Willis. Through his own research and
study, Chris already knew the Canton claim in detail when he asked
to visit the Hall of Fame's archives in the mid-1990s. More impressive,
however, was the fact that the recent college graduate had a well-
developed appreciation for pro football's early years and, through his

research, had come to understand the importance of the period in the genesis and growth of the NFL.

Ah, but an outlet, a venue for the dissemination of this young man's dedicated study, was needed. Impressed by his work, the Hall of Fame introduced Chris to the Professional Football Researchers Association (PFRA). An organization of pro football researchers, scholars, and historians, the PFRA was a perfect conduit. Willis quickly became a regular contributor to PFRA publications and programs.

Chris's interest in and study of pro football history has not only earned him the respect of the Hall of Fame and pro football historians but has also provided history-rich NFL Films with an employee solidly committed to the preservation of the game's all-important heritage. Willis provides NFL Films—pro football's preeminent storytellers—a historian's perspective. And, as evidenced by this publication, he has found new ways to make use of material from the NFL archives.

Willis's constant search for unfound or underappreciated nuggets of knowledge, however, has taken him beyond the archives of the Hall of Fame and NFL Films. He has traveled to places like Portsmouth and Ironton, Ohio, and Mesa, Arizona, to interview aging former players or just about anyone who can shed new light on an old subject. With a keen eye for history, Willis knows what to ask his subjects and how to elicit important recollections and stories that mainstream sports media have missed over the years. Stories like one shared by then-ninety-five-year-old Glenn Presnell, who related how he turned down contract offers from three NFL teams in 1928. Presnell, who later starred for the NFL's Portsmouth Spartans and Detroit Lions, initially passed on the NFL, opting instead to play for an independent pro team in Ironton called the Tanks.

"A man named Nick McMahon made me a contract offer that was the same as the NFL," Presnell told Willis. However, the deal-maker, according to Presnell, was that McMahon also promised him a job as a teacher in the Ironton school system. It was a practice that gave the Tanks' management the ability to successfully compete against the recruiting practices of the NFL.

Presnell's recollections of a bygone era, like many others offered in this book, are priceless. The pro football reminiscences and stories compiled and transcribed for this book by Willis portray an accurate and entertaining look at that all-important "old leather" era of pro football's past. It's a work whose time has come. Here's hoping that someone in the future has the same affection for our present as Chris Willis has demonstrated for our past.

Joe Horrigan
Vice President of Communications/Exhibits
Pro Football Hall of Fame

Preface

A S A YOUNG BOY GROWING UP IN COLUMBUS, OHIO, I DEVELOPED passions for reading and football. No wonder. My family grew up just a few miles from the Ohio State University campus and Buckeye football, and my father owned a used book store. Most of my free time was spent in the sports section of my father's store reading every football book on the shelf. I especially enjoyed reading about the exploits of my favorite teams—the Buckeyes and the Cleveland Browns of the National Football League (NFL). With every page I turned and every book I finished, my passion for the sport grew.

Of course, obsessing about football is not unusual in Ohio, where fall weekends are devoted to the sport. Ohioans turn out en masse for high school games on Friday nights, for the Buckeyes and the state's other small-college teams on Saturdays, and for the Browns and Cincinnati Bengals on Sundays. The state brims with football history and tradition, and nearly every citizen has a football story to tell. That's why I wrote this book.

I was fortunate while growing up to be able to feed my passions for reading and football in my father's bookstore. I'm fortunate now, too, because my job allows me to continue indulging those passions. Since 1996 I've worked in the Archives Department at NFL Films, and my duties include conducting research and occasionally interviewing former NFL players. One of my interview assignments inspired me to undertake this project.

While researching a piece on the league's first-ever playoff game, the historic 1932 indoor battle between the Chicago Bears and the Portsmouth (Ohio) Spartans, I discovered that Spartans running back Glenn Presnell was still living in Ironton, Ohio, near Portsmouth. He graciously agreed to an interview, and on a cold February day in 1999, he spent more than an hour with me sharing, in vivid detail, his memories of the joys and struggles of playing in Portsmouth during the Great Depression.

Presnell's interview inspired me to pursue this project to find players from Ohio's long-gone NFL teams. I wanted to collect and preserve a colorful chapter in the history of Ohio and the history of pro football. My goal was to preserve first-person accounts of pro football in the days before television, when salaries were small, helmets were leather, fields were sandlots, and all the players went both ways.

This was a golden opportunity to hear the history of the game through the people who lived it. There was just one problem. Most of the players from the era when Ohio was the "Cradle of Pro Football," I discovered, were gone. Those who lived and played in the NFL's early days were passing and taking the story of those years with them.

Instead of giving up, I expanded my research and scoured libraries for archival interviews with old-time greats like Hall of Famers William Roy "Link" Lyman (chapter 12) and Earl "Dutch" Clark (chapter 17). Transcripts of those archival interviews, some of them more than forty years old, are published here for the first time.

I also decided that if I couldn't get firsthand accounts *from* the early NFL players and owners, then I would get firsthand accounts *of* the players and owners from family members who knew them best, and from the fans who met them and followed their exploits on the gridiron. Each interview covers a certain aspect of the early pro game; you'll hear stories from former players, fans, owners, a team treasurer, and a league president.

Also, there are stories from almost every town or city that had an NFL team in Ohio during pro football's formative years. Towns and cities such as Akron, Canton, Cincinnati, Columbus, Dayton, LaRue, and Portsmouth are represented throughout each chapter.

This book is the fruit of my interviewing and research. It focuses on the first fifteen seasons of the NFL, 1920 to 1934, years when the NFL grew out of its "cradle," and football, with its reputation as a small-town sport played by roughnecks, changed into a respectable game played by superior athletes before huge crowds in the nation's biggest cities.

This volume is not meant to be an encyclopedic account of those years; instead, it simply tells the story of those who organized, watched, and played in the NFL in Ohio during the league's formative years. Each chapter contains a transcript of an interview I either collected or recorded. Minor errors were corrected, such as dates and scores when memories deviated from the facts. Otherwise, the interviews appear just as they were told. It was not only a challenge but an honor to help preserve these stories and learn about a time in Ohio football history worth remembering.

Acknowledgments

MANY PEOPLE CONTRIBUTED GREATLY TO THE WRITING OF THIS book. At the top I would like to thank Leo Blackburn, Dr. Louis Chaboudy, Norris Steverson, and Glenn Presnell, four great men who gave me their time and energy to help write this book. All four men are no longer with us, and this book is dedicated to them. I'd wished they lived to see their stories in print. They are the true pioneers of professional football.

I thank Scarecrow Press for publishing this book, especially Stephen H. Ryan, acquisitions editor, for believing in this project. I also thank Jessica McCleary, production editor, and the entire Scarecrow staff for their professionalism in getting this book published.

A big thank-you goes out to the individuals I interviewed and the families who helped bring back to life the early days of professional football in Ohio. I owe a debt of gratitude to James and Velda Carr, Irene Cassady, Terri Murdick, Kate Benson, Babe Sherman, and Theresa Graham of Columbus; William Guthery, Sr., and his son Bill Guthery, Shelby Guthery, Jim Anderson, and Bob Lingo of LaRue; Mary Presnell, Bob Vaughn, and Jim Ridgeway of Ironton; Jim Kennedy, Ava Chaboudy, Alma Kahl, and Paul O'Neil of Portsmouth; Mark Fenner, Virginia Kinderdine, James Kinderdine, and Jack Kinderdine of Dayton; Donald and Ann Heslop, Tim Heslop, and Dr. James King of Canton; John Haley of Mendon, Vermont; Margaret Steverson of Mesa, Arizona; and Dr. C. Robert Barnett of Huntington, West Virginia.

In addition I want to applaud the following people for helping me with the writing of this manuscript. Writing an oral history was a very arduous process, and these individuals went beyond the call of duty to help me: Paul Conlow and Rita Benson LeBlanc of the New Orleans Saints; and Craig Heinz, Keith McClellan, Richard Whittingham, and Bob Carroll of the Professional Football Researchers Association. A heartfelt thank-you goes to the Barnes & Noble bookstore located in Moorestown, New Jersey. Most of this book was written there on weekends and in the evenings, so thanks for being open and keeping the food and drinks coming.

I am very grateful for my colleagues at NFL Films, who gave me their advice and support throughout this process: Ray Didinger, Howard Katz, Diane Kimball, Sue Nicholson, David Plaut, Phil Tuckett, Angela Torma, Barry Wolper, and Neil Zender. I also thank Steve Sabol, president of NFL Films, who gives me an opportunity every day to feed my passion for football. I can't think of a better person or company to work for.

In Canton, Ohio, sits the Pro Football Hall of Fame—my favorite place to visit—and I am always indebted to the staff for their expertise and generosity. A huge thank you goes to Pete Fierle, information services manager, and Saleem Choudhry, researcher, of the Hall of Fame research library. Not only do they answer all of my questions—and I usually have a lot—but they also do it better than anyone else. I also want to thank Joe Horrigan, vice president of Communications/Exhibits at the Hall of Fame, for taking the time to write the foreword to this book. I've always considered Joe somewhat of a mentor because nobody understands and studies the history of professional football as well as he does. But I also consider him a friend, who makes every trip to Canton an enjoyable one.

I thank John Haas and Duryea Kemp of the Ohio Historical Society for their help in locating the Nesser Brothers photo and Dr. James King for finding the Lester H. Higgins photo.

Finally, I thank my family, who have supported me and my football addiction through thick and thin. To Jennifer Lynn, my best friend, who, despite your lack of interest in football, was always there to encourage me. Thanks for your ultimate friendship. To my brothers, Rhu and Adrian, the best brothers anyone could have. To my father, Roy, thanks for giving me a place to find my passion and the freedom to chase my dreams. I can't thank you enough. And to my mother, Tina, thanks for your love and inspiration. You inspire me every day to set goals for myself and then go out and achieve them; and for that, I am grateful.

Introduction

From the beginning, the Roaring Twenties lived up to its name. With the world safe for democracy after World War I, the United States discarded its battlefield persona and replaced it with an excess of fun and leisure. Prosperity fueled the celebration. Famed writer Paul Gallico wrote, "We had just emerged from a serious war and now wanted no more of reality but only escape therefrom into the realms of the fanciful."[1] In 1920 prohibition went into effect, American women got the right to vote, radio was popular, Warren G. Harding was elected president, and yes, ten professional football owners gathered in a Canton, Ohio, automobile showroom to organize the American Professional Football Association (APFA). Two years later, they renamed the league the National Football League (NFL).

The NFL was established during the age of flappers, jazz, the Charleston, Lindbergh, speakeasies, Capone, flaming youth, Chaplin, and sports of all sorts. For the first time, the world of sports captured the public's eye and its pocketbook. In the words of one historian, "next to sport of business, Americans enjoyed the business of sport."[2] Most Americans enjoyed the economic boom following World War I and spent a lot on sports tickets as they flocked to stadiums and arenas in record numbers. Sports heroes emerged in every field of athletics. Names such as Jack Dempsey in boxing, Red Grange and the Four Horsemen of Notre Dame in college football, Lou Gehrig in baseball, Helen Wills and Bill Tilden in tennis, Bobby Jones in golf, and Johnny Weissmuller in swimming simply made this the Golden Age of Sports.

Gallico, who followed all the sports giants of the twenties as a columnist and sports editor of the *New York Daily News*, said, "Sports and sports stories and sport characters who were almost magical in their performance provided much of that escape" for Americans to enjoy their free time.[3] Throughout the 1920s, professional football was an unloved child in the family of American sports. Baseball was indeed the national pastime. Baseball occupied the nation's conscience, and the biggest stadiums, and had the biggest name in sports during the Roaring Twenties: Babe Ruth. And if baseball didn't fascinate you, there was always college football. College football had its well-established traditions and its rah-rah attitudes that would make front-page headlines. On the other hand, professional football and the NFL went mostly unnoticed. The sport was truly unloved.

But what was it really like in the early days of the NFL, when the game was played in an era before television, million-dollar contracts, fantasy football leagues, domed stadiums, and field turf? What was the "Old Leather" era truly like, when professional football was fashioned from canvas and leather and played on a dirt field? In *The Football Encyclopedia*, football historian Jordan A. Deutsch explains, "Much of what we know about the early days of pro football has come from the pages of the newspaper of the day. Little is revealed from newsreels and photographs of games tantalize us with frames of action, but cannot tell us of the pace of the game or what it was like to watch. All we have left is our imagination."[4] Let's join Deutsch and attend an Old Leather game up close and personal.

We can get a front row seat for one dollar. If we're at Canton's Lakeside Park to watch the Canton Bulldogs, a mere 4,000 fans would pack the bleachers. A program would cost ten cents. There are no souvenir or beer stands, but you could bring your own liquor flask for later. You could also make a friendly bet on who would win with your neighbor sitting next to you. Usually five dollars would do the trick. Other spectators would be wearing suits and ties, no outrageous costumes with team logos. No cheerleaders or banners to help pump up the crowd. These fans come to see the game, not to be seen.

The field is your familiar 100 yards long, laid out in five-yard segments, with real grass, or more likely, real dirt. It has no hashmarks. Not until 1933 will the ball be brought in towards the middle of the field when a play ends near the sidelines or out of bounds. The bench area is just that, a wooden bench with maybe a bucket of water for a drink at halftime. The goal posts are roughly 20 feet high and stationed at the front of the goal line.

When the teams take the field, we notice that there are only 16 players on each squad. By 1930 the league votes to expand the roster to 20. Most players are paid about $100 a game, while some star players might make up to $150. Both teams wear dark jerseys, giving fans a tough time telling them apart. The uniforms show little individuality, except for maybe a logo or letter on the front. The faded jersey might have a number on the back, but the practice wasn't yet standard.

The trousers are made of canvas, worn with hip, thigh, and knee pads. Each player wears black high-top shoes with rectangular cleats and wool socks, if they had their own socks. The jersey was pulled over a flimsy set of shoulder pads that didn't seem to protect anything. The same could be said for the helmet, which was made from leather and called "head helmets." Some players didn't bother to wear one. No rule requiring a player to wear a helmet was passed until 1943. The NFL in the Roaring Twenties had a rag-tag look to it.

Instead of a whole set of officials, we only see three that govern the action. An umpire, a linesman, and a referee. The officials also keep the game clock on the field, no fancy scoreboards here. From our bleacher seat we see that the ball is made of leather and is fairly round. Easy to drop-kick, but difficult to pass. By the end of the decade the ball is slimmed down, making passing easier.

After a coin toss at the center of the field, we see a kickoff at the 40-yard line. All 22 men who were on the kickoff teams stay on the field, no substitutes. Each man plays both offense and defense. Most plays are called at the line of scrimmage instead of a huddle. The head coach doesn't send in plays and little time is spent in between plays. There are also no television timeouts. Most lineman weigh about 200 pounds, with most backs being much smaller.

Passing was restricted because of the rather fat ball. Some teams passed more than others, but the early pro game was built around the power running game. Also, most rules still handicapped the passing game throughout the 1920's. Until 1933, the forward pass had to be thrown from five yards behind the line of scrimmage. Until 1934 an incomplete pass in the endzone was an automatic touchback and gave the ball to the opponent. Also, most coaches didn't have the time to practice the passing game since most teams only practiced once a week.

Most professional teams used the single wing or Notre Dame box, a predominantly rushing offense. Defensively, most teams used the six- or seven-man fronts to counter the rushing attacks of early NFL teams. Regardless, both offenses and defenses were so close to start a play, that when the ball was snapped 22 men would converge on the ball and after the dust settled we could see the ball carrier usually only gained a few yards.

Punting was the key to the outcome of most games. The way to victory was not to possess the ball, but to give it to your opponent deep in their territory and let him make a mistake. An amazing number of punts occurred on third down, as teams played for field position. With defense so emphasized, low scoring games dominated the early days of the NFL. Some games would end in a 0-0 tie. If you were lucky enough to see a touchdown, you definitely didn't see any endzone celebrations from the players. The game usually lasted about two hours and ended with a gunshot from the referee.[5]

Representatives of pro teams were under the gun in 1920 when they met in Canton, Ohio, to organize what would become the NFL. The pro game was beset with problems: salaries were skyrocketing; players hopped from team to team during the season to play for the highest bidder; and too many teams padded their rosters with moonlighting collegians playing under assumed names. A league needed to be formed.

They had good reason to meet in Canton, now the site of the Pro Football Hall of Fame. Ohio was the geographical center of professional football. Proximity was important in that era when teams traveled by train, and team managers sought games with opponents in cities in Ohio and the Midwest that could be easily reached by rail. Thus, only a few East Coast teams played during the NFL's early years, and the too-distant West Coast would not be home to an NFL franchise until after World War II.

Ohio had the best teams and the best players during the early years of the NFL. Starting with the founding of the NFL in Canton in 1920 through the 1934 season, the Buckeye State was the focal point of the early pro game. *Six hundred forty-five* different men played in nine different cities during that time period. The nine cities in Ohio that had NFL teams were Akron, Canton, Cincinnati, Cleveland, Columbus, Dayton, LaRue, Portsmouth, and Toledo. Four of the first five NFL champions were from Ohio—the Akron Pros (1920), the Canton Bulldogs (1922–1923), and the Cleveland Bulldogs (1924)—and the state earned the nickname the "Cradle of Pro Football."[6]

The historic meeting in Canton marked the birth of the NFL and the beginning of the maturation of pro football. In the following years, the league evolved from a loose association of struggling franchises into a tightly organized, respectable, major sports league. Alas, something was lost as the league grew up. Under the steady guidance of NFL president Joseph F. Carr of Columbus, the league gradually abandoned Ohio's small towns for the big crowds and big venues in the nation's biggest cities. Carr's strategy paid off when the economic bubble burst in 1929, and the Roaring Twenties crashed into the Great Depression. The league struggled, but with a solid foothold in the big cities, it managed to survive through the Depression.

The exodus from the Buckeye State was complete by 1935, and for the first time in its history, the NFL opened the season without an Ohio franchise. The league had finally outgrown its cradle. It was the end of an era in professional football history. The following oral history is an imaginative look at how the state of Ohio and its citizens became the driving force behind the NFL's formative years. This is their story.

Lester H. Higgins

Treasurer, 1919–1923 Canton Bulldogs

[Ralph Hay] had a dream that someday pro football would be as big as major-league baseball.

—Lester H. Higgins

Lester H. Higgins (1889–1981) was interviewed by two Ohio newspapers—in 1969 by the Akron Beacon Journal *and in 1970 by the* Canton Repository. *The two interviews were found in the Canton Public Library.*[1] *Higgins was born in Middlebranch, Ohio, on June 29, 1889, and went on to marry the former Lulu Hay. When Lulu's brother, Ralph Hay, purchased the Canton Bulldogs in 1919, to generate publicity for his Canton auto dealership, he turned to his brother-in-law to help out the team. Higgins worked at the local bank in Canton and became a logical choice for treasurer of the Bulldogs.*

In 1920 Ralph Hay got an idea to start a pro football league. He had heard some rumblings about a league being formed, but nothing was being done. So on September 17, Hay held a meeting in his automobile showroom with owners of the best pro football teams in the country, and they started a pro league called the American Professional Football Association. In 1922 the league changed its name to the National Football League.

The following day, the big sports story in the Canton Daily News *was the signing of Wilbur "Fats" Henry, the All-American tackle from Washington & Jefferson College, to play for the Canton Bulldogs. Only by accident did they mention that a new professional football league was established that same day.*[2] *Higgins was present at this historic meeting and handled the Bulldogs' finances until 1923, when Ralph Hay and the city of Canton gave up the team. Higgins continued to work at the Citizens Savings Association Bank in Canton from 1916 until his retirement in 1964, serving as president from 1957–1963.*

I WAS BORN IN MIDDLEBRANCH, OHIO, LOCATED IN PLAIN TOWNSHIP, about seven miles from Canton. I ended up completing the eighth grade in the Canton school system before getting my first job at Kohler Manufacturing. They made farming tools. I was fourteen years old at the time. I stayed with Kohler for thirteen years before joining Citizens Savings Bank in Canton.

I first got involved with professional football because of my wife, the former Lulu Hay. She was the sister of Ralph Hay, who owned the Canton Bulldogs, and through him I got started in the pro game. Because I worked at the bank in town, he wanted me to handle the financial end of the team. So I was treasurer of the Canton Bulldogs when Ralph owned them. We went along with it for a couple of years until Ralph got out.

Ralph Hay was an automobile dealer. He was one of the early auto dealers in Canton. He sold Hupmobiles and Jordans in a building [at Second Street and Cleveland Avenue] where the post office now stands in downtown Canton. He thought it would be good publicity for his business, so he got in touch with Jack Cusack, who had owned the team prior to this time. He turned the team over to Ralph, including all the contracts with the players and the football park lease. That was before the new league was formed. So Ralph had the Bulldogs starting in 1919. He had all the players who were college stars. They did have one local man, Dutch Speck. He played with us all the time and lived in Canton.[3]

Ralph got the idea he'd like to see a league formed, so he had a dream; I always called it that. He had a dream that someday pro football would be as big as major-league baseball. So he wrote a letter to all the teams east of the Mississippi that had pro football clubs and arranged for a meeting at his salesroom in Canton. He invited all the pro teams. There were twelve or fifteen men there representing the different franchises, and they agreed unanimously to have a league.

They then got to selecting the officers, so they elected Jim Thorpe for president. They wanted Ralph to be the president, but he thought Jim would be more of a drawing card and give the league more prestige. Well, Jim wasn't a businessman and, of course, didn't function that well.[4] They did form the league, and they named it the American Professional Football Association.

Well, I also remember there were automobiles in the showroom. We were sitting on the running boards and chairs because Ralph Hay's office was too small for everyone. We then had several other meetings, mostly in Chicago, to sort out the schedule and player's contracts and things of that nature. The following year, we decided that Jim wasn't producing the way he should, so they elected Joe Carr as president. He was the sports editor of a Columbus [Ohio] newspaper and also ran the Columbus Panhandles pro football team. Carr was the right man for the job. He had the leadership to help the league grow.[5]

Running a pro football team at that time did have its problems. It cost us $3,300 to put a team on the field for a game. When we played on the road, we got a guarantee of $4,000 a game. That was to cover the players, player salaries, and the expense of traveling. In those days, of course, there were no airplanes; we traveled by train in sleepers. When we'd leave, say for Chicago, we'd occupy the whole sleeper. We had eighteen men and the trainer, and we'd take this sleeper out of Canton on Friday night to Chicago, stay the one night, play on Sunday, and come back. It was tough.

Those eighteen men would play sixty minutes, no substitutes. If one got hurt, maybe a tackle would then have to play in the backfield or on the end. They played all sixty minutes. We had a man that played center by the name of Al Feeney. He was from Notre Dame. He played for the Bulldogs for a couple of seasons. He played in one game and got hurt. I went into the dressing room to see him and he had his lip cut. It was just spread apart really bad. He showed me his teeth, which wasn't any better. They fixed him up and he went out and finished the game. They just had to play the whole game, that's all there was to it.[6]

Most of the players were pretty reasonable fellas. They weren't too bad to deal with, contract-wise. They earned it. I remember one game in Hammond, Indiana. They had a great quarterback named Milt Ghee. He tackled Jim Thorpe and it made Jim mad. He said, "I'm gonna get you." He got him and they carried him off the field. He just twisted his neck.[7] He did the same thing to Fritz Pollard, who was a great player for Akron. Thorpe didn't like the way Pollard hit him. So the next time they hit, Thorpe took him out. He was a rough guy.

At this time, there was a lot of betting at these games. They bet their horse and buggies. They bet anything. There were a few fellas that followed us out of town and bet on us. Also, in Canton they'd go along the front of the grandstands with their money in hand and say, "Anybody want to bet?" They'd just hold the money up in the air. Canton fans would do anything at the games.

Sometimes attendance would be a problem. Here in Canton, our field would only hold about 7,000 or 8,000 capacity. When we played Massillon [Ohio], we would have an overflow of people. But we didn't have any reserve seating; it was first come, first served. We'd get about 12,000 people in there. They'd break the fence down and everything. We would lose money because they'd break the fence down and didn't pay. Then there were games when we didn't get any more than a couple of hundred people.

After the 1922 season, Ralph gave it up because it was too much of a drain on his business. He only had it the couple of years. He called all the businesses together in town, and they decided they wanted to keep pro football in Canton. But they needed some money to keep it going, so they agreed on a plan of $1.00 for every employee the businessmen had. That went across real well, and they got the money they needed. When I came into the bank, I got between $45,000 and $50,000 for the team.

Ralph stayed on as a manager, but he let Guy Chamberlin, our great end, run the team for a couple of years [1922–1923], and they won the world championship both of those years. We ended up paying Chamberlin $2,500 per season to be player-coach. But they used up the money, and the businessmen didn't want to raise any more. They moved the team to Cleveland. That was the first time in a long time Canton didn't have a good pro football team playing in the fall. We had a lot of trouble in those days, but who would have thought the league would continue to thrive and become so popular?[8]

After his retirement from the bank, Lester Higgins continued to live in Canton. In October of 1974, the Stark County Board of Mental Retardation dedicated the Lester H. Higgins Adult Center, a workshop for the retarded. Higgins passed away on January 12, 1981, at the age of ninety-one.

Extra Point

Back-to-Back NFL Champions

The Canton Bulldogs were the first team in NFL history to win back-to-back world championship titles in 1922 and 1923. They finished those two seasons with a combined record of 21-0-3. They still hold the NFL record for Most Consecutive Games Won Without a Defeat with twenty-five (twenty-two wins, three ties). To show how dominant they were, the Bulldogs outscored their opponents 430 points to 36 in those 2 seasons. The 1923 Bulldogs gave up just 19 points in 12 league games and surrendered just 1 touchdown all season—a touchdown run by Cleveland Indians fullback Johnny Kyle on November 25. The Bulldogs still won that game 46-10.[9]

Joseph F. Carr

NFL President, 1921–1939

He obviously had a love for sports in general, but his first love was not baseball and not basketball, but football. He loved it.
—James Carr, grandson of Joe F. Carr

Joseph F. Carr (1879–1939) was born in Columbus, Ohio, on October 23, 1879, the son of Irish immigrants. Then a pioneering executive not only in football, but also in basketball and minor-league baseball, with only a few years of formal education, he became a sportswriter for the Ohio State Journal. He was also the manager of the Columbus Panhandles professional football team before becoming the second president of the American Professional Football Association in 1921. The following year, he helped rename the fledgling organization the National Football League. James Carr, the grandson of Joe Carr, was interviewed by the author for an hour on September 14, 2002, at the Pro Football Hall of Fame in Canton, Ohio.

Carr served as president of the NFL for eighteen years (1921–1939) and helped football become a more stable and respected sport in the eyes of the public and the media. During the first several years of his presidency, he introduced a standard player's contract to help control players' hopping from one team to another. He made peace with the colleges around the country by establishing a rule that prohibited any NFL team from signing a college player until his class had graduated. He also recruited financially stable team owners in big cities, bringing the game to bigger crowds in bigger venues. He patterned this idea after major-league baseball, thinking this was the only way the young league could survive.

The NFL was fortunate to have Carr's leadership ability in those early years to help guide the league. His passion and love for the sport until his death in 1939, while he was still in office, were obvious. In 1963 Carr was named one of seventeen charter members of the Pro Football Hall of Fame.

MY GRANDFATHER ALWAYS HAD A GREAT AFFECTION FOR THE CITY of Columbus, and that dates back to the fact that his father, my great-grandparents, who were Irish immigrants, came to Columbus in the mid-nineteenth century. He worked here, and they raised their children here. There were seven children in the family. My grandfather was one of four boys and two sisters. Most of them stayed in Columbus and made it their home. The Carrs became very comfortable here, not only for the families, but for their church, too.

My grandfather ended up living in Columbus at 1863 Bryden Road. It was a double. It was a very modest home. They didn't have a lot of fancy furniture or items like that. They lived a pretty modest life in Columbus. My grandfather was a pretty small man physically, probably about five feet five inches, along those lines, but his personality and heart was what separated him from others. He was pretty conservative—a very ethical, very religious, and spiritual man. He brought those qualities to the National Football League. He also was a very gregarious man. Whenever there was a gathering of any sort, church or league meeting, when he entered the room the place would light up because he was such a dynamic man. He had a certain charisma about him that I think helped him in his work. He would go around and press the flesh and say hello to everybody. He would ask how they were doing. He showed a general concern to everybody, which was very impressive—that he was concerned about other people. Regardless of who they were, he would show interest in them.

As he was getting started in his career, he would be gone from his family for a while. He was dedicated to the NFL. When you're on a path, on a venture of getting a league started, you have to devote most of your time to that goal. So he was gone a lot. But he had a great relationship with his two children—with my father, his son, Joe Carr, Jr., and his daughter, my aunt, Mary Carr—who he just adored. I think the fact that his children idolized him gives a good indication that the time that they did spend together was quality time. They also created ways to see him. Sometimes the family would go down to the railroad tracks near home, and when the train was passing, my grandfather would go to the back of the caboose to where the railing was and wave to his children, and they'd wave back. It was a small thing, but it meant a lot.

I think in those early days before he did anything, he had a natural love of sports and he wanted to be involved. As a youngster, he became a machinist at the Pennsylvania Railroad, and he saw these men, huge men, working as boilermakers in the Panhandle Division. These men were named the Nesser brothers, and they were rough and tough guys.[1] So he decided to ask the railroad if he could develop a professional football team. So that's how they started the team and how he got going in the football business.

He also got involved in sportswriting with the *Ohio State Journal*. He used his newspaper experience to help promote the Nesser brothers and his team, the Columbus Panhandles. The reputation of the brothers being hard-nosed football players and the team working for the railroad was a perfect match for my grandfather. It made it easy for them to be successful. The team was mainly a traveling team because one of the perks for working on the railroad was that they could ride for free anywhere, so it saved the team from traveling costs and cost to rent a field. So Columbus never really saw the team play, but the various towns elsewhere, especially in Ohio, got to know them really well.

The Nesser family had a lot of contact with my grandfather. He had a lot of affection for the Nesser brothers. After all, they were the mainstay for all those years. The brothers kept the Columbus Panhandles going all those years. He might not have had the career that he did if it hadn't been for the Nesser brothers. They spent a lot of time together at practice, and on the train rides back and forth from games. They became very close, and he held them in the highest esteem.

My grandfather also got involved in other sports, too. He obviously had a love of sports in general, but his first love was not baseball or basketball, but football. He loved it. He helped organize the minor-league system in baseball and already saw major-league baseball become a major sport, so I think he saw the potential for professional football. He's been quoted as saying, "I can see the day when professional football will be the biggest sport in America." So he had the ambition and the vision to stick with football and help develop it. That's what he did.

Through his experience with the Panhandles and baseball, he became a first-rate administrator, and pro football was in need of some leadership. So in 1921 the American Professional Football Association hired my grandfather as league president to replace the great Jim Thorpe, who was an athlete, not an administrator. But that was my grandfather's area of expertise. At that time, they needed somebody with a good business sense to help develop the league.

He ended up taking a very low salary, which wasn't important to him. He had a love for the sport and the new league. He didn't want to take any more than he felt was fair. So he asked the owners, and they agreed to have the league run from 1921 to his death in 1939 in downtown Columbus, Ohio, in a modest building numbered 16 East Broad Street. That's where the NFL was run—not New York, not Chicago, not the big city as one might think; it was in his hometown of Columbus.[2]

As soon as he took office, he started making changes. The first thing he had to do was prevent players from team-hopping. You would have a ringer on one team one week, and then he would be on another team the next week because somebody offered him five dollars more. He wanted teams to have more stability, so he came up with the standard player's contract, similar to baseball. If you have players signed to a contract, then things became more predictable and players would stay with one team. This took a couple of years, but by the end of the 1920s, teams became more recognizable. Fans in cities could go out and root for their team. Johnny Unitas was the quarterback of the Baltimore Colts and so forth.[3] That's what the rule eventually helped establish for the NFL. Fans now had something to root for, as opposed to the ringers who would jump from team to team. That situation became confusing; it was chaos. I think my grandfather saw, from the fan's point of view, that there would be much more popularity if there were much more predictability.

He also came up with a rule that players could not play professional football until their class had graduated from college. This rule was put in when Red Grange left college after his last college game [in 1925]. This rule also helped ease the relationship between the pros and the universities, which was needed at that time. The rule encouraged players to stay in school, get their education, then go on to play pro football. There were several situations where certain players were in rather desperate situations and they needed to go to the NFL, and they challenged the rule. He sometimes agonized over those decisions, but he always stuck to that rule. I think he had to.[4]

He had the attitude that this was a young league, and he had certain rules and regulations. If you strayed from them or made exception after exception, that would undermine the continuity and strength of the league. He was given the power to enforce these rules, and if he wanted to exclude somebody from the NFL, he could do that. I think the owners backed him most of the time in these decisions and gave him that power to exclude people or enforce those regulations. For example, at one time the Green Bay Packers had been fudging on the rules [using college players in 1921], and my grandfather said, "I know most of the teams have been fudging on this particular rule, but this is the first time I've caught somebody in this infraction." So he pulled the franchise from Green Bay for some time, which had to be tough. He was pretty hard-line on most of the decisions, but the owners and players knew this. They knew their actions would have consequences, and I think that basically motivated him.[5]

My grandfather had a great relationship with all the team owners. He and George Halas of the Chicago Bears had a tremendous mutual respect for each other. Sometimes they had differences of opinions, and that bothered my grandfather, but they always respected each other. He knew my grandfather had the expertise to run the league and was comfortable in him handling any situation. All the owners felt that way. Also, they were all very close friends. He was good friends with Art Rooney of Pittsburgh. He was very good friends with Tim Mara of New York. He was friends with George Preston Marshall of the Washington Redskins. He had a special bond with those owners.[6]

I think that deep friendship that developed between my grandfather and the owners led to the type of trust in which they felt, OK, Joe, you're the man. You have the experience. You can do the job. Go ahead and do it and you're not going to get interference from us. That's why he was able to stick to his guns on the rules and regulations, because he had the owners' support. There was a trust built up due to those friendships.

Besides building these friendships with team owners, he helped put franchises in the big cities away from the smaller towns which started pro football. He saw that the opportunity was there for pro football to become a major sport, and the only chance it had to succeed was to be played in the big cities. There were tough times early on, but as time went on, the league started to grow and showed signs of potential. That's because it had a firm foundation, and, moving from the firm foundation, it became bigger and bigger. It didn't happen overnight, but it eventually happened. It's kind of interesting that the last game he ever saw was the 1938 NFL Championship Game in New York. The number of fans that were in the seats exceeded 48,000 people, which had to be gratifying to him, especially before his death from a heart attack in May of 1939.

My grandfather had his first heart attack in 1937, and back in those days, there was little that they could do for people except for nitroglycerin. I think after that heart attack, it took a toll on him. He had a stressful job, but the fact that he loved it so much I think would take away that feeling of stress. Prior to his first attack, he was a very heavy smoker of cigars and that sort of thing. We know today that can take a toll on your heart. Also back then, during that period of time, what they told you to do was, basically, do nothing. Just rest. So he tried to rest as best he could, but it developed more in the next two years, and it finally took his life.[7]

It amazes me how he and the owners not only formed the league but cleaned it up and made it what it is today. I am also so incredibly honored that he is inducted in the Pro Football Hall of Fame. It just amazes me because very few people have that privilege of having their likeness and the deeds that they have accomplished live on through a museum. When I saw my grandfather's bust there, it was a fantastic moment for the family—one I'll never forget.

On September 14, 2002, I attended the Nesser family reunion, which was being held at the Pro Football Hall Fame. I was delighted to be there and have the opportunity to meet the generations of relatives of the Nesser brothers. It was a wonderful event, and to witness the Columbus Panhandles display with the Nesser family was special because of what the family meant to my grandfather.

I'm kind of shocked that people of such reputation as the Nesser brothers and my grandfather have been pretty much ignored by the city of Columbus. When you walk into City Hall, there are pictures of people who are relatively unknown—mostly politicians [rather] than the city's famous citizens. So I am a little disappointed that they haven't honored him. He's in the Pro Football Hall of Fame. He was the president of the NFL for over eighteen years. He also was head of the baseball minor league system and helped start a professional basketball league. He was a pioneer in the early years of professional sports. You would think that Columbus would want to honor a man with such accomplishments. But it hasn't happened yet. I'm amazed.

I think he hasn't been remembered because time has gone by, and generations have come and gone. The people who used to know him are mostly gone. I think that's one factor. Maybe the people in power would do something to commemorate my grandfather, but maybe they aren't aware of him. I hope it's that. Columbus is a very conservative town, and I think a lot of their attention in the football area is focused on the Ohio State Buckeyes. That's their mainstay.

We like Columbus, and our family continues to love sports—all of us. My [physical] stature is more like my grandfather's, so I wasn't very successful in playing football, but I love the game. One of my greatest loves is watching Ohio State on Saturdays, yelling and screaming at the TV set and so forth. My brothers, Dennis, Gregory, John [who has since passed away], and Michael, will be there, too, cheering on the Buckeyes. We've stayed close as a family, and I think that's important.

As I said earlier, I'm amazed at the things he did and his tenacity, his hard work, and his absolute love of football and the NFL. I've always had a tremendous amount of respect for my grandfather, especially because he was a pioneer in this area, so I have a huge amount of respect and love for him.

Joseph F. Carr died of a heart attack in Columbus, Ohio, on May 20, 1939, at the age of fifty-nine. He was inducted into the Pro Football Hall of Fame as a charter member in 1963. James Carr is an attorney who lives in Columbus with his wife, Velda. Joe Carr's other grandsons, Gregory, Dennis, and Michael, also live in Columbus.

Extra Point

No to Branch Rickey

In 1935 Branch Rickey, the man who broke baseball's color barrier by signing Jackie Robinson, was the general manager of the National League's St. Louis Cardinals. He made Joe Carr an offer: "If you give up football," Rickey said, "I'll make you the biggest man in baseball."

"If that's the price I'd have to pay," Carr replied, "I'll have no part of it."[8]

Fritz Pollard

Halfback, 1920–1921, 1925–1926
Akron Pros; 1922 Milwaukee Badgers;
1923, 1925 Hammond Pros;
1925 Providence Steam Rollers

> Being black never really affected me on the playing field. I was taught
> early on by my father and brothers not to pay any attention to anything
> negative.
>
> —Fritz Pollard

*Frederick "Fritz" Douglas Pollard (1894–1986) was interviewed at his
home in New Rochelle, New York, on June 24, 1976. The forty-five-
minute interview was found in the archives of NFL Films. Pollard was
born on January 27, 1894, in Rogers Park, then a primarily white neigh-
borhood on Chicago's North Side. His father was a barber who was
born in the West Indies, his mother was an American Indian, and he and
his brothers excelled both in music and athletics. After a stellar high
school football career, Pollard eventually ended up at Brown University,
where he made football history.*

*Pollard was a true pioneer because he became the first black back-
field player ever elected to Walter Camp's All-American team in 1916. In
January of 1916, he became the first black player to play in the Rose
Bowl, where his team from Brown lost 14-0 to Washington State. Pollard continued his list of firsts when he went on to play professionally,
as he became the first black head coach in National Football League history in 1921 for the Akron Pros. With the help of co–head coach Elgie
Tobin, the Pros went 8-3-1 and finished in third place. Pollard also
played in 1921 and finished tied for second in the league in scoring with
42 points. Pollard played in forty-nine NFL games over six seasons.*

*He also played several seasons for a couple of independent teams in
the Pennsylvania coal region. After his playing career, Pollard became in-*

*volved in many business ventures including running a newspaper, be-
coming an entertainment manager, and running several all-black pro
football teams. He was inducted into the College Football Hall of Fame
in 1954.*[1]

M Y PARENTS MET IN OKLAHOMA. AT THAT TIME, MY FATHER, WHO
was from the West Indies, was going to school and worked at
the local barber shop. My mother, who was a full-blooded Indian, fell in love with him. My father learned the barber trade fairly early
and continued that profession for a long time. Shortly after getting married, they moved from Oklahoma to Illinois to a part of town near
Chicago called Rogers Park. Rogers Park was an all-white neighbor-
hood, and I think living there helped me later in life.

While living in Rogers Park, my father opened his own barber shop,
while my mother became a seamstress. Because of my father's connections
at the barber shop, my mother got a lot of work with the top department
stores in Chicago. My other siblings and myself were born there, and I really looked up to my brothers while growing up, especially Luther Pollard.
I can remember our father teaching us how to pitch, and Luther went on
to become a great pitcher, as well as a great football player when he played
at Lakeview High School. He later went on to star at Dartmouth.

The other brother I looked up to was Hughes Pollard. He was the
musician of the family. We both learned to play several instruments from
our father, which led us to play in the school band as well as athletics.
He continued his love of music throughout the rest of his life. It was
Hughes who got me to play football in high school while the both of us
attended Lane Tech. See, the coach wanted Hughes to play very badly,
but when Hughes saw that I wasn't there, he asked the coach, "Where's
my kid brother? You haven't given him a chance to play." Hughes was
the head of the school's orchestra and was very popular in school, so the
coach respected him very much. Because of that, the coach gave me a
chance to play football in high school. At that time, I only weighed about
ninety pounds.

I was real excited about playing organized football. I used to play a
lot of pickup games with my brothers during my grammar school days.
They made sure I got a chance to play despite my size. They taught me
a lot about the game. I remember my first game in high school against
Hyde Park. They tried to massacre me. But my brother Hughes told
them, "That's my kid brother," and because they had so much respect for
him, they didn't give me any trouble from then on.

Being black never really affected me on the playing field. I was
taught early on by my father and my brothers not to pay any attention

to anything negative. I just eliminated that kind of thing from my mind. I would forget the color of my skin when I played, and if anything happened to me physically, my brothers taught me how to protect myself. See, opposing players would try to hit me hard, one on top and one below. But my brothers taught me to spin out of it, so I wouldn't get caught in a pileup where they could get me. After that, some players would say, "Well you little black so and so, I'll get you the next time." So the next time they'd tear into me again, but after the tackle I would spin away from them. That was a way of protecting myself against any rough play.

I ended up playing four years at Lane Tech and became All Cook County in Illinois. Since my brother was a very popular player at Dartmouth, everybody thought I would follow him there. So I enrolled, but after a few weeks, I decided to leave. That's when I decided to go to Brown University. It was rough there for awhile, but I finally made the football team. After the 1915 season, we were asked to play in the Rose Bowl against Washington State [January 1, 1916]. We played on a muddy field, so I wasn't that effective, and we lost 14-0. The next year, I made Walter Camp's All-American team. But then I started losing interest in school and decided to leave.

At this time, I didn't have any knowledge of professional football until my friend, Clair Purdy, who played quarterback at Brown with me, asked if I was interested in playing. He got me an invite to play for a team in Akron, Ohio. My first year in pro ball, I weighed only 160 pounds. I was playing against giants out there. I must've looked like a midget. Clair Purdy told them a whole lot about me before I got there because the whole team respected me when I arrived. That was very nice of him, and I felt very welcomed. As for playing, Purdy was going to make a star out of me, which he did. He gave me a lot of opportunities to run with the ball. That was fine with me.[2]

The Akron team I joined was good, but far from a polished team. Most of the players would come in on Sunday morning to play a game that afternoon. That was typical of most pro teams. When I first arrived in Akron, I made my way to [Akron owner] Frank Neid's smoke shop, where the team would meet.[3] The manager would say, "Well you better get out there and learn the plays and signals." We would have practice at 11:00 a.m. before the game. This was two hours before kickoff, so I had to go out there and learn everything in about an hour. I was fortunate to have Purdy there to help me. We ran a lot of plays we learned from playing at Brown.

The coach of the Akron team was a guy named Elgie Tobin from Penn State. I didn't like the plays he had, so that's why we started to run the Brown system. I think the only other team in the pros that was running our system was the Canton Bulldogs. I found that out when we played against them later in 1919. We started to win games, so the whole team accepted the change, and the Akron management loved it.

I didn't have any problems playing with Akron. They adopted me very well. On the football field, they blocked for me and everything else. I think it wasn't any different than Jim Thorpe and Pete Calac [both Native Americans] playing in Canton.[4] The town would cheer for me. Akron was a very southern-like town. Some southerners came up to work here when the war [World War I] started, but when I played, they would cheer, "We want Pollard! We want Pollard!" So I never had any trouble. Throughout that year [1920], the team treated me right, and I had a lot of respect for them. I had a good year, and I made a lot of long runs, which helped us win the league championship.

The next year in Akron, I thought I could make the team better by recruiting a few players. The biggest name I got was my good friend Paul Robeson, who also was another early black player. I became friends with Paul while I was at Brown and he was at Rutgers. So I talked him into playing for Akron, and the team accepted him. He played that season with us, but his main interest was singing. I used to play the piano for him, and he would sing. He was a great singer. I think he could have been a great player had he not gone into show business.[5]

Akron's biggest rival at that time was the Canton Bulldogs. When I first came to Akron, I didn't know where Canton was. I ended up meeting some people in Akron who took me to Canton so I could play. Naturally, I heard about the great Jim Thorpe, but I imagine he had heard about the great Fritz Pollard since I had a name at that time too. Jim was really a fine fella. I think there was a lot of propaganda built up about those Indians. But they were good fellas. I used to kid them all the time about me having as much Indian blood in me as they did because of my mother. They enjoyed hearing it.

I remember one time we played Canton, and Jim came out before the game and said to me, "Hello little black boy." I said, "Hello big black boy." He gave me this stunned look. He was dumbfounded. He didn't expect me to return an epithet like I did. I then said, "Well, we're going to play against each other and will find out who's going to be the blackest after this game." Jim laughed. He then called the other two Indians over, Joe Guyon and Pete Calac, and introduced them to me.[6] Fortunately, Akron won the game, and I happened to be the star of the game. Jim and myself became pretty friendly after that.

The players who played back in my days were pretty rough. They were mostly sandlot players. Then they started to get better college players and paying them better. But it wasn't until Red Grange came into pro football that it got some much-needed publicity and respect. There were some people who thought Red wasn't as great as the publicity made him out to be. But he was. I should know because I played against him. He was a great player. Everybody in pro football should be grateful for him and what he gave to pro football. From the time Red Grange came in, pro football kept on growing. It was one of the great things for pro football.

I played several more years in the NFL with teams in Milwaukee, Hammond [Indiana], and Providence. I also played several games in the Pennsylvania coal region near Gilberton. Those fellas would work all week in the mines, then come out and play football on the weekends. Some of them resented the fact that a college man would come out and play, but after you played a couple of games, they would become more friendly. They respected me because I knew the game. In the beginning, it was a little tough, but when they saw you could play, they accepted you.

It was the same off the field, too. In the beginning, they wouldn't accept you. So what I did was offer them to come out and get a drink. I didn't even drink, but I would say, "Come on, fellas, and let's get a drink." They look at me strange, then after awhile they finally warm up. Little by little they would come out. First there would be one, then two or three the next time. They would start to loosen up. It was just a case of knowing how to handle the situation and having them come out and be your friend. I think that helped me become a better player because they would play harder and block harder.

I had a lot of fun playing pro football. I got a chance to play the game when you played all sixty minutes, while today, you have an offensive team and a defensive team. Unless you got seriously hurt, they wouldn't take you out. I liked the era I played in. I think I'm a very fortunate man because I'm eighty-two years old now [1976], and I'm still able to get around. I'm very thankful that I had a chance to play professional football.

Fritz Pollard passed away on May 11, 1986, in Silver Spring, Maryland, at the age of ninety-two. Pollard's achievements long ago as a pioneering black player and coach have not been forgotten. In 2003 a group of coaches, scouts, and front-office personnel formed the Fritz Pollard Alliance to promote minority hiring in the NFL. Then on February 5, 2005, Fritz Pollard earned pro football's ultimate honor by being selected to the Pro Football Hall of Fame, some seventy years after his last pro football game.

Extra Point

APFA First Champions

If you look in the *NFL Record and Fact Book*, you will see the Akron Pros listed as the first champions of the APFA in 1920, the forerunner to the NFL. But nobody on the Akron team was celebrating because the league didn't officially award the title to Akron until the spring meeting the following year. So on April 30, 1921, the Akron Pros were officially declared the champs. I guess that hometown celebration had to wait.[7]

Nesser Brothers

Every Position, Pre-NFL
Columbus Panhandles,
1920–1922 Columbus Panhandles

> Getting hit by a Nesser is like falling off a moving train.
> —Knute Rockne, end for the Massillon Tigers

In the history of the National Football League, there have been over 240 brother combinations in professional football. But no family has produced more than the very athletic, gifted, yet underappreciated Nesser family. There were six brothers who played in the NFL: John, Phil, Ted, Frank, Fred, and Al. A seventh brother, Ray, also played a few games but not in the NFL. No other family in the history of the game can claim that many siblings. The closest would be the Browner family, who had just four. Also on the team were a brother-in-law, John Schneider, and a nephew, Ted Hopkins. You would think the number would stop there, but in 1921 the Nesser family once again made NFL history. During that season, Ted Nesser played with his son Charlie. They become the first and only father-son combination in NFL history. Truly a remarkable family.

On September 14, 2002, the Nesser family had their annual reunion at the Pro Football Hall of Fame; 168 family members attended the reunion. While at this reunion, five Nesser descendants—Irene Cassady, Terri Murdick, Theresa Graham, Kate Benson, and Babe Sherman—were interviewed by the author.

THE NESSER BROTHERS WERE THE SONS OF THEODORE AND KATHERINE Nesser. Theodore moved the family from Germany to the United States shortly after the Franco-Prussian War of 1870. He was drafted into the war and saw action, but he was wounded, losing part of his finger on his left hand. Because of his dislike for the wars that were going on in Europe, Theodore was determined that none of his children would ever fight in one, so he moved his family to America. He came over first with his brothers, and then Katherine followed. She came across the ocean by herself with five kids. They would eventually settle in Columbus, Ohio.

The Nesser family would eventually grow to a total of twelve children—eight boys and four girls. Being German immigrants, the boys picked up sports as a way to fit in and exert their energy. The eight boys consisted of the two oldest, John and Phil, who were born overseas, Ted [the first one born in America], Fred, Frank, and Al. These were the six brothers who would go on to play professional football for over thirty years. The seventh brother was Raymond, who would eventually play a few games with the brothers, then went on to become a police officer in Columbus. The eighth brother was Pete, who despite being 350 pounds never played football. The game never appealed to him.

There also was a brother-in-law, John Schneider, who went on to marry Rose Nesser. Then we had a nephew, Ted Hopkins, who also played. Usually, there were at least eight or nine Nessers playing at once. It was truly a family affair.

The Nesser boys grew to be very big kids. Most of them were over six feet tall, with Fred being the biggest at six feet five inches and about 250 pounds. This was unusual because the parents were both slight in stature. Theodore was about five feet seven inches, and Katherine was only five feet one or five feet two. She was a little rotund but certainly not obese. She ran a tight ship, and those boys were scared of her. They weren't frightened of each other, but they were scared to death of her. When they would get into arguments when they were kids, they would get into some serious fisticuffs. They'd have a knock-down, drag-out fight, and they'd better be in the backyard when they did it. She would let them go at it for awhile until one of them drew blood. Then she would grab a clothes prop or a mop handle and would beat them over the head until they stopped fighting. They were kind of hostile, yes, but they loved each other dearly. They got along very well. They were no different than any other siblings.

Growing up in Columbus, the boys went to work fairly early. None of them attended college, but they could've. Thus, they all ended up working in the Panhandle Division of the Pennsylvania Railroad. This is where they met Joe Carr, a fellow employee who also had a passion for sports. Carr started a baseball team and then formed a semipro football team [1907] with workers from the railroad. They called themselves the Columbus Panhandles. He built the football team around the six Nesser brothers. Even though Carr was a big sports fan and administrator, football was always his first love. At this time, pro football wasn't very popular and was not well organized. But Carr had two advantages to make his team successful. First, because his team was comprised of workers on the Pennsylvania Railroad, they could ride the train anywhere for free. Thus, Carr saved a lot of money on travel expenses. Because they traveled for free, Carr scheduled mostly road games. While on the road, he would advertise the team around the six Nesser brothers. They became a big attraction for out-of-town teams. The Panhandles franchise would go on to travel and play professional football for almost twenty years.

The brothers would do everything together. It was such a large family, they usually made their own fun. I think that's how they got started playing football. They heard about the game, and then they would go out and play on the railroad yards during their lunch hour. This would be the only practice they would get. They would eat for fifteen minutes and then practice for the remaining forty-five. If it rained, they would stay inside and play cards, mainly euchre. They prided themselves on playing nineteen games of euchre on their lunch break. So it was pretty quick; you had to keep up. But this is where they learned to play.

On the few occasions they played a home game, they would play at old Recreation Field in German Village. The field was located at the corner of Whittier and Yeager where the Big Bear [grocery store] is now. They would usually play a local team from Columbus at this field. The team would have enough players, but sometimes the Nesser boys wouldn't know who they were playing with. See, everybody knows there are eleven players on a team, and there were six brothers, a nephew, a brother-in-law, and sometimes Raymond. That makes nine. They didn't know where the other two came from, but they would play. Sometimes Rose Nesser [sister] would drive them to the field. She would load them all up in the wagon and drive them to the field. This is how she met her husband, John Schneider.

Traveling was always fun for the brothers. They would work during the week from seven in the morning until four in the afternoon. Then they would work from seven until noon on Saturday and then take off on the train to wherever they were going to play. They usually got there in time to play on Sunday. If they arrived early into town, they would usually find a barn to sleep in to save some money. After the game on Sunday afternoon, they would head back home just in time to go to work at seven on Monday morning.

Sometimes in these different towns, they would leave some opposing players pretty banged up. That didn't leave the fans in a good mood. Many times the fans would be running towards the moving train with sticks in one hand and rocks in the other, wailing at the team. The fans would get very upset with the Nesser brothers or the Panhandles team for beating up their players. They were very physical when they played. They were brutal players. They weren't honed in the college ranks, but by playing in the yards at the railroad. That was their brand of football. It's what made them famous and such a popular drawing card in the early years of professional football. One newspaper account said after a Panhandles game, "They may not have won the game, but they went away with less bruises." This was typical reporting for a Panhandles game. Many newspapers would point out the physical play of the Nesser brothers. Here are a few famous headlines:

"The Nesser boys are heavy and fast, and when one of the Nesser boys hit you flush, there is usually a little work for the water boy and the club doctor."

—*Detroit Free Press*, 1915

"The Columbus outfit is headed by six Nesser Brothers. Big huskies who are easily the equal of the best football players ever turned out by the biggest universities in the country."

—*Ft. Wayne Journal Gazette*, 1915

"Ted plunged through the Tiger line time after time with as much ease as one would shove a hot knife through butter. He bowled over tackles, shook them off, carried four or five before he was downed."

—*Massillon Independent*, 1916

"Once again the presence of the Nesser Brothers guaranteed injuries."

—*Detroit Free Press*, 1916[1]

The most famous quote about the Nesser brothers came from Knute Rockne, who played end for a few professional teams. He said, "Getting hit by a Nesser is like falling off a moving train."[2] They always said that Ted Nesser had the same nose as Knute Rockne. They really did have the same nose. As a matter of fact, Ted had his nose broken eight times. Our family doctor, Dr. Charles Turner on Mt. Vernon Avenue, told Ted he wasn't going to set his nose anymore because he would just break it again.

Sometimes their brutal play wasn't limited to opposing players. You see, sometimes when an opposing team didn't have enough players, they would take some of the guys off the Panhandles team and let them play for the opponent. Most of the time, it would be John

Schneider, the brother-in-law. John would say, "I was the poor fool they would choose. I was scared to death. Usually, I couldn't work for a week. They would just pulverize me. They were mean. They were mean as bears." John would also say he didn't know what was scarier: playing against the Nesser brothers or asking them to marry their sister. That was a toss-up.

They could have killed a man on the field, yet they were gentle as lambs off the field. They each had their own families and their own children. They always had time to play with the kids. I think that was another unique thing about them. They could leave a man lying on the field all bloody and bruised, but they would be very gentle and sweet away from it. They were special in that way.

The brothers loved their families, and they loved to compete. They didn't play for the money. So you know it was for the love of the game or to get away from their wives, one or the other. I know later, when Al and Frank played in the NFL, they would get paid maybe two hundred dollars or three hundred dollars for a game. They thought they were rich. I wonder what they would think of some of the salaries today. Unbelievable. I know Ted used to say they were born fifty years too soon.

From 1909 to 1919, right before they joined the National Football League, the Columbus Panhandles compiled a record of 48-39-7. That wasn't too bad, considering they played most of their games on the road. By the time they joined the NFL, the team and the Nesser brothers had played almost fifteen years of football. They were a little too old to compete successfully in the NFL. I think this hurt them. Most of their success was before the NFL was established. Al Nesser did make some All-Pro teams from 1922 to 1925. But I think this is why they haven't received much recognition.

Even in the city of Columbus, they haven't been honored. You have to remember Columbus is a college town [Ohio State University], and that's all right. We are all Ohio State fans. We had a few of our uncles play there.[3] We will always be Ohio State fans, but it would be nice to see the city do something to honor them. Part of it is the city doesn't know much about the Nesser brothers or Joe Carr. I think you could walk up and down High Street in downtown Columbus and ask 1,500 people who the Nesser brothers are and they wouldn't know. That I think is sad because we did play a big part in the history of Columbus.

They were a bigger-than-life family. It's a family dream, but we would be thrilled even with a partial realization of it. I think to have a permanent marker or street would really validate what the family accomplished in those early years of professional football. We would be able to see it, and it is so much easier when you can see something and touch it. You get the idea of what it was they did and who they are. It would be nice if the city did do something, but we won't be broken-hearted. The Nessers will go on.

On September 14, 2002, we had our annual family reunion at the Pro Football Hall of Fame. We thought this would be a great site to have the whole family meet and learn about the contributions they made to pro football. It was also a great chance for the younger generation to mingle with the older generation. We thought it worked out really well. Even though no Nesser brother is inducted into the Hall of Fame, there is a nice display of the family in the exhibition area where the first 100 years of pro football is honored. In this display, they have a Panhandles football, a Panhandles blanket that used to belong to one of the brothers, and a couple of photos. One of the photos is of the whole family. It's a great display. I mean, how many people get the opportunity to see pictures of their whole family from that far back, let alone in a place like the Pro Football Hall of Fame? It gives you a little thrill to see them and know so much about them.

Having our reunion at the Hall of Fame made our family feel wonderful. But I did shudder a little bit about being in a room with 168 Nessers because they will all talk. By the end of the night, we all had aches from our heads to our toes from laughing. It was a fantastic time. Everybody was into learning about the family's history. It has been great to see the younger generation get involved and carry on the tradition. We have some of the young boys playing high school football, and some are coaching. That night, I thought it was great to say you're part of the Nesser brothers or the football team. But I think it's even greater to say, "Yeah, I'm a member of the Nesser family because there's a lot more to them. They are a good group of people."

No other family has sent more brothers to the NFL than the Nesser family. All six brothers are now deceased, but their legacy lives on. The city of Columbus has never recognized the family in any way despite their early contributions to pro football.

Extra Point

The Oldest Nesser

John Nesser of the 1921 Columbus Panhandles became the oldest player to ever play in an NFL game at the age of forty-five. In later years,

Bobby Marshall of the 1925 Duluth Kelleys and Ben Agajanian of the 1964 San Diego Chargers tied the NFL record. (Gary Anderson of the 2004 Tennessee Titans became the fourth player to participate in an NFL game at the age of forty-five.) But it wasn't until fifty-two years later, on September 23, 1973 (Oakland Raiders hosted the Miami Dolphins), that George Blanda broke the record. Blanda went on to play until he was forty-eight years old, which remains an NFL record.

George "Hobby" Kinderdine

Center, 1920–1929 Dayton Triangles

When Hobby traveled to games, he always made sure to carry his Bible
and send a telegram back to his wife saying he was fine.
—Virginia Kinderdine, the daughter-in-law of George Kinderdine

*George Kinderdine (1891–1967) was born on August 13, 1891, in Mi-
amisburg, Ohio, and attended Miamisburg High School. He didn't play
football in high school or college. He started playing organized football after high school and later joined the Dayton Triangles semipro football
team in 1917. He continued to play with the Triangles until 1929, the last
ten years the Triangles (1920–1929) were a member of the NFL.*

*He also had two brothers who played with him on the Triangles
team: Walt and Harry Kinderdine. The Triangles folded after the 1929
season, and George retired from the NFL. He continued to work at his
job with General Motors in Dayton. Virginia Kinderdine, the daughter-
in-law of George, was interviewed for forty minutes by the author at her
home in Miamisburg on June 7, 2003. Also present were the grandsons
of George Kinderdine: Jim and Jack Kinderdine.*

MY FATHER-IN-LAW WAS BORN IN MIAMISBURG, OHIO, IN 1891 AND
attended high school there. For whatever reason, he didn't
play football in high school. He learned to play football on
the sandlots of West Carrollton and Dayton. He loved the sport. When
he got out of high school, he went to work for a company in Middle-
town that made safes, like the ones in banks. After a few years, he went
to work with General Motors in Dayton. He stayed there until he retired.

At this time, he started playing semipro football in Dayton. He played with the Dayton Gym-Cadets in 1915. Then, when the Cadets changed their name to the Triangles, George joined them. The Triangles team was made up of employees of three local businesses operated by General Motors: Dayton Engineering Lab [renamed Delco], Dayton-Wright Aeroplane Manufacturing, and Dayton Metal Products. That's where the Triangles name comes from—the three companies. The team would practice and play its games at Triangle Park.

In those early years, he idolized Jim Thorpe. He [Thorpe] was his hero. He would always keep a photo of Thorpe in his wallet, even after he retired. Several years into his playing career, he got a chance to play against Thorpe. He always thought it was a thrill to play against him. Then in the 1920s, he was asked by Thorpe to play with him in some postseason exhibition games. He always enjoyed that.

I ended up marrying George's only son, James Kinderdine, in 1937. James would tell me how he would accompany his father to practice down at the park. He would watch his dad and the other Triangle players go through their drills. Once during practice, George hurt his ankle and hobbled around for a couple of days, so the team started to call him "Hobby," and the nickname stuck for the rest of his life.

Hobby only weighed about 165 pounds, and he played ten years in the NFL. What a feat. Two of his brothers also played: Harry "Shine" Kinderdine was a guard, and Walt Kinderdine played in the backfield. Harry got his nickname because he was a shoeshine boy while growing up. He then went on to become the sheriff of Montgomery County. It was special for the boys to play together.[1]

Hobby had a great relationship with all his teammates, especially Sneeze Achiu. Sneeze played at the University of Dayton and then came to the Triangles in 1927–1928. The two of them stayed friends even after playing professional football. I remember watching Sneeze wrestle around Dayton. I would be scared that he was getting beat up pretty badly, but when we all went out for dinner afterwards, he looked like he didn't have a mark on him. This was professional wrestling, and they sure knew how to hide it.[2]

When Hobby traveled to games, he always made sure to carry his Bible and send a telegram back to his wife saying he was fine. He made sure his family would not miss him. He only made one hundred dollars every Sunday plus expenses. That was his pay for the whole ten years in the NFL. One hundred dollars a game. He loved the sport.

In 1920 when the Triangles joined the NFL, Hobby made history. On October 3, 1920, the Dayton Triangles played the Columbus Panhandles in the first-ever NFL game. In that game, Hobby kicked the first-ever extra point in NFL history as the Triangles won 14-0. The city of Dayton can be proud that it hosted the first-ever NFL game. I know the Kinderdine family is proud that it was involved in that game and the contribution of Hobby.[3]

I think the memory of the Triangles in this area is fading away a little. I don't think the community as a whole is as aware of the Triangles' history as they should be. There used to be a sports writer in Dayton by the name of Si Burick who used to write many articles on the old Triangles team and its players. But when he died, there wasn't much being written about them.[4]

When the former Triangles were living, they cherished the years they played. Each year the team would hold yearly reunions. The former players would meet and tell old war stories. It was fun for them. They were all very close. When Hobby passed away in 1967, several of his ex-teammates came to his funeral. I think there were about seven of them. That was very nice to see. He was such a great person, not just football-wise, but as a person. I couldn't have asked for a better father-in-law.

George Kinderdine played center all ten years (1920–1929) that the Dayton Triangles were in the NFL. He passed away on June 22, 1967, at the age of seventy-five. His daughter-in-law, Virginia Kinderdine, stills lives in Miamisburg, Ohio. Her two sons, Jim Kinderdine, who played football at Kentucky and now lives in Yorkville, Indiana, and Jack Kinderdine, who played football at Dartmouth and now lives in Centerville, Ohio, also work for General Motors.

Extra Point

Triangles' Greatest Game

In 1921 the Akron Pros appeared to be on their way to a second league title after winning the 1920 APFA championship with an 8-0-3 record. They started the 1921 season with a 7-0-1 mark, improving their unbeaten streak to nineteen games (15-0-4). Then came the game on November 20 against the Dayton Triangles at Triangle Park. A highly contested battle ended with a Russ Hathaway field goal in the third quarter and a Triangles 3-0 victory.[5] The Pros never recovered, losing their next three games and finishing in third place. The Triangles completed the season with only four wins in 1921, but they did have the biggest win in team history that season.

CHAPTER **6**

Lee Fenner

End, 1920–1927, 1929 Dayton Triangles; 1930 Portsmouth Spartans

Most of the Triangles players were paid one hundred dollars every Sunday. Doesn't sound like much, but back then that was a lot of money.
—Mark Fenner, great-grandson of former
Dayton Triangles end Lee Fenner

Lee Fenner (1898–1964) was born in Dayton, Ohio, and ended up playing football and basketball at Dayton Stivers High School. Instead of going to college and playing football, he decided to go to work at Delco, a division of General Motors in Dayton. He went on to play for some of the company's sports teams, including the Dayton Triangles football team in 1916. The Triangles went on to be a charter member of the American Professional Football Association in 1920, the forerunner of the National Football League.

Fenner played eight seasons with the Triangles in the NFL and one game with the 1930 Portsmouth Spartans. Fenner retired from pro football after the 1930 season but continued to work for Delco until he retired. Mark Fenner, the great-grandson of Lee Fenner, was interviewed by the author for an hour in Dayton, Ohio, on June 8, 2003.

MY GREAT-GRANDFATHER WAS BORN IN DAYTON, OHIO, AND STAYED here his whole life. He graduated from Stivers High School, which was a co-op school. He got a lot of manual training there, and that helped him get a job with Delco right out of high school. Delco was a division of General Motors. He had offers to play college football at several eastern schools including Cornell, but in the end he decided to stay close to home and go to work.

He went to work at Delco, and in his spare time he started playing with the company football team. Like most of the players on the company team, he learned to play football from pickup games around town. He ended up playing a lot of sandlot games down near Wolf Creek in Dayton. Later when he played in the NFL, he got a little tired of answering the question from other players and sportswriters: "Where did you go to college?" So instead of saying he didn't go to college, he would say, "I played at Wolf Creek Naval Academy." That answer went over well, so he would say it all the time.

In 1916 the company team changed its name from the Dayton Gym-Cadets to the Dayton Triangles, and they played under that team name until they disbanded in 1929. My grandfather played end on the team during those years. He was always known for his speed. I've heard he ran like he had razor blades in his shoes. He caught a lot of passes, too, in a day when not too many teams threw the ball. The Triangles had a quarterback by the name of Al Mahrt who was one of the better passers in the game, so they liked to throw the ball.[1]

Lee was also known as a fierce tackler, even for his size. He was only about five feet ten inches and 170 pounds, but he was a tough guy. In 1920 the Triangles played a classic game here in Dayton against the Canton Bulldogs with Jim Thorpe. The Triangles weren't a very big team, and the only way they could tackle Thorpe was with one man high and one man low. Then they would kick him, bite him—anything they could to get him down. That was the game in which Thorpe came off the bench and kicked two late field goals to salvage a 20-20 tie with the Triangles. That was a moral victory for the Triangles.

Most of the Triangles players were paid one hundred dollars every Sunday. That doesn't sound like much, but back then that was a lot of money. They deserved every penny of it. Not only were the games hard, but the traveling they had to do on trains and buses was a tough chore. The Triangles were mainly a traveling team; the company thought it was less of a gamble to play on the road. The guarantees from teams in big cities like Chicago and New York sounded pretty good to the team managers, so they became mainly a traveling team.

When they did play at home, they would play at a field called Triangle Park. It wouldn't hold more than 5,000 or 6,000 at full capacity. Today, the park is still there and called Triangle Park. A full baseball diamond sits where the football field used to be. But it is nice to know that the field is still there, and athletic contests are still being played there. Also, a shed is still there, and we believe it is the old locker room that the team used when playing. We're still looking into it, but we believe it is the original one.

The last home game at Triangle Park was in 1927 against Red Grange's New York Yankees on October 2. A week earlier, the Triangles defeated the Frankford Yellowjackets [6-3], and the team was feeling pretty good about facing Grange. A couple of days before the game, the *Dayton Daily News* had an ad promoting the game. It was going to be a big game for the city of Dayton. Unfortunately, the Triangles lost the game 6-3 before a crowd of 6,000.[2]

After the Yankees game, the Triangles tied the Yellowjackets in a re-match game. Then they would go on to lose seventeen straight NFL games from 1927 to 1929. After the 1929 season, the Triangles were sold to a group of businessmen in Brooklyn. When the team was sold, it broke my great-grandfather's heart.[3] He did play one game with the Portsmouth [Ohio] Spartans in 1930 but retired after that. Later in life, he never watched any more football games. I guess the Triangles' folding left a bad taste in his mouth. He thought the current game was wimpy. He couldn't watch a bunch of overpriced athletes playing with plastic helmets. He just didn't like watching it.

All of the knowledge I've learned of my great-grandfather has come by doing research over the past five years. Until then, I knew he played football, but I didn't really know anything. In my research, it amazed me—the athletes he played against, like Red Grange, and the venues he played in. I didn't know he played at the Polo Grounds, Cubs Park, which is now Wrigley Field. He played in these great venues. So now, all of a sudden, he and the Triangles became more of real thing, as opposed to just a sandlot team that played in someone's backyard.

Despite my great-grandfather's dislike for the game, I think the city of Dayton is slowly learning about the history of the Triangles. Very few people around Dayton understand the true history and significance of the team and how they contributed to the early years of the NFL. They were a charter member of the NFL in 1920. This was the founding of the NFL, and the Triangles played in the league that first year. That's worth remembering.

The city is now working on a project called the Carillon Historical Park, which has a goal to educate the community on the history of the area. One part of the project will focus on the athletic achievements of the teams and its players, which the Triangles will be a big focal point. I'm in charge of gathering the Triangles' history for the project. This will go a long way in preserving the Triangles history. Also, in 1999 a web-site was established by Steve Presar just on the history of the Triangles. That has helped further the team's history and traditions.[4]

The city is starting to learn about the team. I know I'm proud of the accomplishment of the team and my great-grandfather in those early years of the NFL. It's also been a discovery time for me and my family. To be able to uncover my family's history has been well worth the time and energy spent doing it.

Lee Fenner passed away in 1964 at the age of sixty-six. His great-grandson, Mark Fenner, is an employee at Miller Brewing Company and lives in Dayton, Ohio.

Extra Point

Carl "Scummy" Storck

Carl L. Storck was a former player and the longtime manager of the Dayton Triangles. In 1921 he became the secretary-treasurer of the NFL and served in that capacity until 1939. When NFL president Joe F. Carr died in May of 1939, Storck took over as league president for two years. A character in the early days of the NFL, Storck could be seen on the Triangle bench smoking a cigar and chewing on his Maude Miller candies. But nobody can explain how he got his nickname, Scummy. I guess nobody wanted to know.

CHAPTER 7

Ike Roy Martin

Halfback, Pre-NFL Fort Wayne Friars,
Pre-NFL Canton Bulldogs,
1920 Canton Bulldogs

> I played pro football because I loved it. I loved anything that was a con-
> test, and football was certainly a contest.
>
> —Ike Roy Martin

Ike Roy Martin (1887–1979) was interviewed in Canton, Ohio, on June 17, 1976. The twenty-five-minute interview was found in the archives at NFL Films.

Isaac Roy Martin was born on July 15, 1887 and was raised on his family's farm in Liberty, Missouri. He went on to play college football for William Jewell College (in Missouri). In 1914, while visiting Fort Wayne, Indiana, he joined the Friars, a local professional team then stocked with ex–Notre Dame players. Martin then followed other Friars players to Canton in 1917 and joined the great Jim Thorpe on the Canton Bulldogs. Despite being a very good ballplayer, he played under assumed names for most of his career. In Fort Wayne it was "Mr. Johnson," and in Canton it was "Mr. Brown."

Martin played on the 1920 Bulldogs team that finished in third place with a 7-4-2 record in the newly established American Professional Football Association. He retired at age thirty-three after the 1920 season. After his playing career was over, Martin continued to live in Ohio.

I WAS RAISED IN LIBERTY, MISSOURI, ON MY PARENTS' FARM. I LIVED ABOUT three and a half miles from the famous James boys. I saw Frank James many times around town while growing up. I mainly worked on the farm, as my family had a pretty large farm. We had about one hundred acres of corn and one hundred acres of wheat. Any free time was spent playing games. I remember in grade school, we would play all kinds of games, and actually, that's where I got my training to be an open-field runner. I always thought anyone with that type of running experience should be better than the fella that hadn't had it.

After graduating from Liberty High School in 1906, I played at William Jewell College in Missouri. When I was playing in college, I gained an awful lot of yards. They said I did it by my unusual "rural" strength. My legs were developed due to the farm work. There was a fella at William Jewel who was a state champion in the 50- and 100-yard dashes. I was kidding around one day with him, and I just said, "You just wait till opening of track season. I'm going to beat you in the 50-yard dash." I don't know why I said it. But I beat him in the 50-yard race and the 100-yard race, so I must've had some speed.

In my early days in college, I seldom wore a helmet, but later I took it up. I'm inclined to believe that the hard material that they use for padding today is the cause of so many injuries, plus the fact I don't believe they are in as good a shape as we were back in those days because we had to be in shape in order to play both offense and defense. I played one whole season, both offense and defense, and never called time-out. A man hardly makes a run today when he has to take time-out to catch his breath. The player today doesn't play enough to be in as good a shape as we were in.

After leaving college, I didn't play any football until I was visiting my girlfriend in Fort Wayne, Indiana, in 1914. While visiting her, the town was talking so much about football down at the local cigar store, I became interested. Most of the men at that cigar shop were posting and taking bets. So I asked them if a person could get a tryout with the club. Well, it was a short time after that, they brought the coach of the Fort Wayne Friars in to see me. We talked a bit. I told him who I was. I told him I would like to play, but I didn't want to play under my own name. He actually knew me because he was from Missouri and saw William Jewell play. So he got me a uniform, and I went out that afternoon and played in the game. That's how I got started in pro football.[1]

I took the name of Johnson. The reason I used an assumed name was most people were opposed to pro football, especially the colleges. Even some industries were opposed to pro football at that time. I took the name so that I'd be sure not to lose my job. I began coaching at Heidelberg College [Ohio], so I didn't want to lose that job. Then the press tabbed me as "the mysterious Mr. Johnson."

Shortly after they were advertising me as Mr. Johnson, we were playing some team; I think it was Wabash [Indiana]. I made quite a few spectacular runs that day. After the game, I had $235 handed to me. Undoubtedly, there were a few fellas that had bet on the game. Then a little kid jumped up on the running board of the car as we were in the parking lot. I was going to the hotel to re-dress, and the kid says, "I know who you are. But I'm not going to tell anyone." I say, "You do?" He says, "Yes I do." And every time he sees me after that he says, "I'm not going to tell anyone." So finally I said, "How do you know who I am?" The kid says, "My brother was here from St. Joseph, Missouri, and he saw you play. But I'm not going to tell anyone."

I knew what he was talking about because at William Jewell College, I had played in St. Joseph a couple of times. That taught me one thing: if you're a star athlete, you're an idol of the youth. Every star athlete in the world owes something to the youth. It taught me to be more careful in what I did in front of the kids.

The Fort Wayne team I played on was pretty much made up of former Notre Dame men. They had Al Feeney, Cap Edwards, Gus Dorais, Pepper O'Donnell, and Knute Rockne. Rockne was an assistant coach at Notre Dame then. Now, Rockne was not a great player. He undoubtedly must've been a great coach, but he was only an average end. He wouldn't have even been a good end if he hadn't had a man like Dorais throwing the ball to him. They always played together.

After playing a couple of seasons in Fort Wayne, some of the players started to migrate to Ohio. I think it was Al Feeney who went first, but it was Cap Edwards who got me to come there to play.[2] He wanted me to play. I was getting older, so I didn't know if I wanted to keep playing. I think 1917 was the first year I played with the Canton Bulldogs, and I played under the name of Brown. I continued to play with the Bulldogs until 1920. At the age of thirty-three, I played my last season with the Bulldogs. I knew we had a good club from knowing the personnel that we had.

The Bulldogs had great players such as Pete Calac, Joe Guyon, Dutch Speck, Cub Buck, and of course, Jim Thorpe. Thorpe was coach and captain. I think Thorpe has been very much misrepresented. He was a great person. Some writers used to depict him as a drunk. But in playing with him three or four years, I never saw him take a drink until after the last game I played with him in Buffalo [1920]. I really admired him. He was always pulling tricks—a likeable fellow.[3]

I remember playing a game in Canton against Akron. It was a tough game, and Thorpe was back catching punts and returning them. One time when they were punting, Thorpe told me to let Nash go by. Bob "Nasty" Nash was a great end. Tough. But Thorpe wanted to run into Nash. They were both knocked out, and they carried them both off the field.[4]

34

If he could avoid it, he wouldn't let you tackle him from the side. Thorpe wouldn't let you. You had to tackle him straight up. He'd run in such a way he made you tackle him straight up. You'd think you had him tackled, then his knees would come up and you get a double blow out of it. I'm sure if there was such a thing as the greatest, Thorpe was it.

I played football because I loved it. I loved anything that was a contest, and football was certainly a contest. I had a desire to be good, and I think without that desire, you'll fall short.

Ike Roy Martin passed away on July 20, 1979, in Aurora, Ohio, just five days after celebrating his ninety-second birthday.

Extra Point

Scoring, What Scoring?

During the NFL's infancy years, scoring points was a very difficult thing to accomplish. From 1921 to 1930, in that 10-year span, the league saw 475 shutouts. In 1926 alone, 75 of the 116 games (.656) played by the 22 teams in the NFL involved a shutout.

Arda Bowser

Fullback-Tailback, 1922 Canton Bulldogs, 1923 Cleveland Indians

Played four times, all sixty minutes with no time-outs, played offense and defense. We had to do both. We didn't have any oxygen on the table. No hand warmers, nothing but a bench to sit on.

—Arda Bowser

Arda Bowser (1899–1996) was interviewed on April 22, 1994, at his home in Winter Park, Florida. The ninety-minute interview was found in the archives of NFL Films. Bowser was born on January 9, 1899, in the Pittsburgh suburb of Danville, Pennsylvania, the son of a preacher. After a stint in the Navy during World War I, he went on to attend Bucknell University. After college, Bowser played on the 1922 Canton Bulldogs that went on to win the National Football League championship with a 10-0-2 record. That season, the Bulldogs scored 184 points and gave up only 15 while winning 7 of those games by shutouts. The following season, Bowser played for the Cleveland Indians, which finished in fifth place with a 3-1-3 record. After the season, Bowser decided to get married and retired from pro football. Bowser was inducted into the Bucknell University Sports Hall of Fame in 1979 as a charter member.

I THINK YOU'RE BORN WITH CERTAIN GENES, LIKES, AND DISLIKES. I HAPPEN to be one of the guys who liked the outdoors. I especially liked playing games. I was fortunate in growing up across the street from a vacant field. It had plenty of space to play games for my two brothers and sister. My father was a preacher, so he had to read and study. He didn't like a lot of noise in the house. He'd chase us outside, rain or shine, to take the noise out with us. That suburb of Pittsburgh where I grew up was very hilly, and we would play run sheep run, camelback, baseball, and whatnot.

That love of games continued in high school as I played all kinds of sports. Then I went to Bethany College in West Virginia, but I was there for only three months in 1917. That year the war broke out, so I decided after the football season I would enlist. After Christmas I enlisted in the Navy but wasn't in for very long. When I got back, I decided not to go back to Bethany. I didn't like the school particularly, and my father and mother had graduated from Bucknell, and my cousin was going there, so I decided to attend Bucknell.

I played at Bucknell for coach Pete Reynolds, and he had a simple philosophy of "Don't get hurt. Get up and keep on going. If you get injured, we'll take you to the hospital," which I didn't care for, so I always got up and kept on going. Coach Reynolds always worked us very hard, sometimes for two or three hours on the practice field. But he was preparing us physically for sixty minutes of football, and if you didn't do it that way, then in the last quarter, you don't show up very well.

Coach Reynolds also didn't believe in hot showers. We had to take cold showers. He thought hot water softened muscles, so he wouldn't let us take hot showers. In November and December, that water comes under those ice cakes up there. It's pretty damn cold.

We weren't allowed to go to fraternity dances till after the season. Pretty strict rules. Before we started the first day of practice, he'd blow his whistle and we'd all get around him. He'd say, "These are the rules fellas. Room check nine o'clock," so on, and so on. He read them off, and these rules had to be obeyed. We had a good end. Buckner was his name, and we just had a big game against Lafayette, our homecoming game. His fraternity was having a dance that night, and he asked Coach if he could go, even if he could just sit in a chair and watch for a while. He told Buckner not to go near the house. He didn't want any of us to be tempted. Just stay away from the fraternity house.

After my second season of football in 1920, I was going home for Christmas, and the train was making a stop. I forget where, but the state students were standing there waiting to board. They were talking about their football team. They were proud of the football team, and I never saw that angle of it before—that the students wanted you to win. Of course, the alumni do. So I went on home with that in my mind—that when I go back there to Bucknell next fall, I gotta win for the students as well as myself.

I always felt that what I had as an athlete, God gave to me. All I had to do was go down on the field and use it. One day, a freshman came into my room the year I was captain. I was very modest about the thing. After visiting awhile, he asked, "How's it feel to be the hero on campus?" That kind of startled me because I never felt that way, and I never heard anybody tell me I was a hero on campus. So I told him that God gave me my talent, and all I had to do was go out there and use it.

I played according to the rules. I played hard, and, as captain, I had a lot of responsibilities. We played to win. We were very disappointed when we didn't. I think my best skill was kicking. I was a good drop-kicker, and my coach helped me get better with what I think was the first kicking shoe. Coach Reynolds said, "Well, let me have your kicking shoe, and I'll see what I can do with it." He took it down to the shoe-maker, and they sprayed off the toe and tacked a piece of leather on the end. The leather had to be thick because of the hard cleats. The shoe was heavy, but it made a buffer between my big toe and the ball. Not only did I get more distance with the shoe, it protected my toes.

Coach Reynolds came up with a lot of crazy ideas. We played Syracuse once, and one of our tackles, John Dooley, had a cracked rib. It was an important game, and we needed him to play. Coach had a fellow down on Market Street in Lewisburg, who ran a grocery store and meat shop, cut a real thick piece of round steak and take the bone out of the center. He gave the steak to Coach, and we taped that round steak to the side of the broken rib and put a pad on top of it, a hard pad to protect it. It did a pretty good job. I heard him a couple of times say, "Uhh!" when he got hit.

At this time, I started to hear about professional football, but most of the colleges objected to the pros using their best players before they graduated. The pro teams would take them out of school, then after a while, they didn't go back. Most of the reporters said that pro football wouldn't go over—that it didn't have the razzle-dazzle that the college game had. They didn't have the girls or band and so forth. That was true. As the quality of play showed up, gradually the pros won over. Today there's room for everyone.

I suppose the major motivation to play pro ball was the money because I was in love and wanted to get married, and this was a good way to hasten it. After I graduated from Bucknell, I signed on to play some games with Frankford near Philadelphia. Then I went to Canton, Ohio, on a visit, and I needed a haircut. I went down to the barber shop, and this guy was cutting my hair, and the plate glass mirror up there had a schedule of the Canton professional team and where they were going to play. This was in August before the season started.[1]

Well the barber was clipping away, and I read the schedule and said, "Who owns the Canton Bulldogs?" He said, "Look across the street, that automobile agency. There's a man looking out the window in the display room. That's Ralph Hay, the manager." I said, "Thank you." When he finished cutting my hair, I walked across the street, introduced myself, and in fifteen minutes I had a job.

Ralph Hay was a businessman. I guess he thought he'd take a chance with me. My contract was done over the phone. Everything was done over the telephone. He had me sign a contract later. The contract I had with Philadelphia was all verbal. We didn't have any agents or lawyers. It was done verbally most of the time—a handshake and that was it. Your word was good.

The day I arrived to play in Canton, Ralph Hay handed me a bunch of three-by-five index cards with the plays and the signals on them. To start the game, I wasn't in the starting lineup; I was just sitting on the bench learning the numbers and the plays. After that I started the rest of the way. We used the single-wing formation, which wasn't too complicated to run. It wasn't deceptive. It was power, power, power.

So in 1922 I coached at Bucknell during the week, then on Friday night hopped a train from Lewisburg [Pennsylvania] to Philadelphia and played in Philly on Saturday, then take a train out of there called the "Cincinnati Express," which went through Canton and then down to Cincinnati. I would catch that out of Broad Street Station, and I'd get into Canton at about six in the morning and play there. I would eat at the Elks Club with some of the other players. That's where they cashed our checks. We were all paid by checks. Most of us cashed them before we got out of town. Sometimes they weren't any good, but that wasn't true of Canton. I'd then catch the 8:00 p.m. train back to Harrisburg, get off there, and take another train north to Bucknell.

There were no airplanes, just slow trains, and if you're six foot two, those old-fashioned booths, which were only about six feet, weren't too comfortable. Your hair would get stuck in the chair at one end and your toes at the other. So sometimes, sleeping wasn't too good. But I was making some extra money, so it was worth it.

I remember once I played in four straight games in four days. Late in 1922, I was scheduled to play my regular game in Philly on Saturday. Then my friend Joe Costas called me to see if I wanted to play in Mt. Carmel [Indiana] on Friday, the day after Thanksgiving. I said I would. But then I get a call from the Philly team saying they had scheduled a game for Thanksgiving Thursday, so I thought about it. That would be four games in four days with my Canton game on Sunday. I thought about it and thought about the extra money, so I agreed to do it. I kept my word and went to Philly on Thursday, took the train and played in Mt. Carmel on Friday, took the train back to Philly, played on Saturday, then took another train all night to Canton, and played on Sunday. Played four times, all sixty minutes with no time-outs, played offense and defense. We had to do both. We didn't have any oxygen on the table. We had no hand warmers, nothing but a bench to sit on.

One game I was paid in one-dollar bills. I had $150 all in one-dollar bills. After those four games, I finally got back to Lewisburg on Monday and went straight to the bank. I went up to the teller's window and handed him my money. He said, "You must've been lucky in that crap game." I said, "It wasn't crap. It was hard work." But I think I had around $1,500 in cash deposited.

Money was always tight. Once there was an advertisement in a Canton store window saying that the first Canton player to score got a new pair of Stetson shoes. I was a poor boy and I needed shoes, so I told our quarterback what I was going to do if we got close for that first score—I would kick a field goal, and I would get the shoes. But there was a lot of competition for those shoes. Some of my teammates wanted them, too, but our quarterback was going to help me. It was raining at the start of this game, so we had a hard time moving the ball. But we finally got close enough, and I kicked a field goal for the first score. I won the shoes.

I played in Cleveland the following year [1923], and that was the year I had a kicking exhibition with Jim Thorpe. Thorpe was playing with the Oorang Indians, and we both took it seriously. We concentrated on the job we were to do, so we didn't chatter back and forth when we were kicking. When the whistle blew to start the game, we got the kids to pack the balls, and we went back off the field. That was it. The next day they didn't write up much about it—you know, him being there and kicking. But they would advertise it before the game to try and sell more tickets. I don't know how many more tickets they sold. Nobody in Cleveland knew me from Adam, but they knew Jim Thorpe.[2]

Watching Thorpe drop-kick was amazing. He seemed to be able to kick off any surface. A dropkick had to just touch the ground. If you got a little grass to work with, what was the ball going to do? Is it going to tilt the ball, or is the dirt going to affect it? So it was very unpredictable. Timing was very important. Thorpe had it down to perfection. I think he could have done it with his eyes closed.

Thorpe was a terrific football player. He was strong. He was agile. He was brainy. You put that and his natural athletic skills together, and he could succeed in any sport. He loved football. If he had a good agent who would have looked after him morally as well as athletically, he'd have been a terrific hero in this country. He played hard, but he played clean. I never knew of him to get into a fight. Of course, I only played against him twice, but we never had any trouble with him. In fact, we'd mingle with him in the hotel rooms. He was very unhappy because he couldn't get his Olympic medals back, and he couldn't get a job coaching. He knew he couldn't play football all his life.[3]

It was a shame they took his medals away from him from the 1912 Olympics. One time I went to Canton for a reunion of Bulldogs players. I think it was about 1960. Thorpe was deceased, but Pete Calac and Joe Guyon were there. So I went to see Joe in his room at the hotel, and we had a nice visit. I asked him about Thorpe playing baseball in the summer that caused him to lose his medals. Joe told me the reason they did it was that the U.S. government would pay Indian students' travel expenses to and from the reservation for their summer jobs, but they didn't feed them, so they had to do something to eat. Thorpe and another Indian went down to this little town in North Carolina and played some sandlot baseball. I think they got fifteen dollars a week or something. It was a very minimal amount. You wouldn't really call it professional. This Olympic guy latched onto this and took away Thorpe's medals. He was a pro because he got some lunch money down there. They never gave Thorpe back his medals, which he wanted. His heirs got them after he died.

Thorpe was a God-made animal, but was a clean player. Most of the Indians were. We were playing Thorpe's Oorang Indians once, and our captain, Duke Osborn, got in the dirt section of the field, and he started to throw dirt in the face of Long Time Sleep. He only took it for so long, and finally he took off after Duke. Osborn ran up the field around the goal post and down the other side of the field. There was a gate at the end of the field, and the Canton cop held the gate open for Duke, who ran through it, then he closed the gate. Finally, the Indians calmed down and allowed us to put Duke back in the game and promised not to cause any trouble. Duke claims that Long Time Sleep was choking one of our ball carriers. Years later I was sitting in my living room listening to the radio and, to my surprise, this radio show is describing this Indian on the warpath at a football game. I knew exactly what they were talking about. I was there. It was the *Ripley's Believe or Not* radio show.[4]

Another time, Jim Thorpe made a contract to take his Indians to Chicago to play George Halas's Bears. But Halas made Jim promise that they have eleven Indians, but at the last minute, Jim couldn't get eleven. We had a fellow on the Canton team, Cecil "Tex" Grigg. He had these high cheekbones, so Jim sold him on the idea of letting him paint his face up to look like an Indian. So he paid Grigg to come to Chicago and play as one of the Indians. Halas didn't know any better, and Thorpe had his eleven Indians.[5]

A few weeks after that, we were playing a game against the Bears, and Ralph Hay wanted me to bring an extra backfield man because we

were short one that week. I told him that I would get him one. I thought
I could get Doc Elliott from Frankford to play on Sunday. So I got in
touch with Doc, and he said he would be delighted to help out. Well,
playing in Chicago, there was only one way out of Philadelphia, and that
was to catch the Pennsylvania Broadway Limited train. To do that, we'd
have to miss half of the fourth quarter of the Frankford game on Saturday. We got the OK from the Frankford man, who grudgingly agreed.
We said, "If we don't have the game on ice, we won't go." I don't know
what we would have done if we didn't go because Ralph Hay would've
been in a hell of mess if we didn't show.

So we made arrangements for the taxi guy to leave our civilian
clothes in the cab and wait for us at that gate. When the middle of the
fourth quarter arrived, we ran over to the sideline coaxing the Frankford
manager to let us go, but he made us run a few more plays, then he let
us go. We ran out the stadium through the gate and into the taxi, told
the driver to give it all he had because we were running a little late. We
pulled the shades down in the taxi to change out of our uniforms and
into civilian clothes. That wasn't a very easy thing to do—changing
clothes in a taxi without a shower.

We pulled up to the curb of the station and got out and ran to catch
the train, which was about to leave. We yelled at the redcap, "Hold that
train! Hold that train!" He held the train for us. Then the train was three
hours late getting into Chicago, and we didn't get to eat breakfast. Hay
met us at the station at about a quarter to twelve. He was glad we made
it, but he didn't know how close it was.

Pro football made me a little money, but I had to make a decision. I
knew I wanted to get married, and now I could see the possibility of
making that happen. It was a disappointment to quit playing football at
that time because I still had some years athletically in me. But I took mar-
riage seriously. You take a vow when you get married to honor her and
keep her as long as you both shall live. I knew that was my primary ob-
jective, and that took priority over football. I played football because I
liked it. I had good luck with it. I had some minor injuries, but the Lord
gave me an excellent body to play.

*After retiring from football, Arda Bowser worked for the White Motor
Company, Penn Mutual Life, and finally with National Life Insurance
Company. He passed away on September 7, 1996, in Winter Park,
Florida, at the age of ninety-seven. In 1994, while celebrating its seventy-
fifth anniversary season, the NFL honored Bowser, then ninety-five, as
the league's oldest living player. Later, NFL officials discovered that
Ralph Horween (1921–1923 Chicago Cardinals), then ninety-nine, was
still living in Virginia.*

Extra Point

1923 NFL Game of the Year

On November 25, 1923, Bowser's Cleveland Indians, with a record of 3-0-3, hosted his old team, the undefeated 7-0-1 Canton Bulldogs. A season high of 17,000 fans showed up at League Park (Dunn Field) in Cleveland to witness the NFL game of the year. Unfortunately, the home-town Indians didn't show up to play, as fullback Wallace "Doc" Elliott scored three rushing touchdowns, leading the Bulldogs to an easy 46-10 victory.[6]

Art Haley

Tailback-Wingback, 1920 Canton Bulldogs, 1921 Dayton Triangles, 1923 Akron Pros

He always told the story about how he lost his two front teeth playing pro football. He seemed to be proud of that.
—Ann Heslop, the daughter of Art Haley

Art Haley (1895–1946) was a star quarterback at the University of Akron and played three seasons in the NFL with teams from Canton, Dayton, and Akron. Ann Heslop, the daughter of Art Haley, was interviewed by the author for an hour at her son's home in Canton, Ohio, on August 1, 2000.

Art Haley was born in Beaver Falls, Pennsylvania, and as a youth moved with his family to Northeast Ohio. He and longtime friend Bruce "Scotty" Bierce became outstanding four-sport athletes at Cuyahoga Falls High School in Akron. The pair went on to star at the University of Akron—Haley as quarterback and Bierce as an end. After college, Haley joined the Bulldogs as a backup for Jim Thorpe, while Bierce played for the Akron Pros. In 1979 he was inducted into the Sports Hall of Fame at the University of Akron.

MY FATHER WAS BORN IN BEAVER FALLS, PENNSYLVANIA, AS AN ONLY child. When he was a youngster, his mother wanted him to become a doctor. She was very protective of my father. Once when he was playing in high school, he got injured on a play and was down for several minutes. Well, she jumped the fence that was around the field and went out there to see if he was all right. She also made my father take music lessons, which he didn't really like. He liked to play sports, and that's what he did. He didn't get too comfortable in Beaver Falls because his family moved him to Ohio when he was young.

As a teenager, my father became friends with Bruce "Scotty" Bierce, who he would end up playing football with in high school, college, and pro ball. They spent a lot of time together playing sports. They continued that later in life, also. They would play golf and handball when they retired from football. They both starred at Cuyahoga Falls High School. My father was the quarterback, and Scotty was the end. They had a great time playing together. They both played football, baseball, basketball, and track in high school. He seemed to be busy all the time.[1]

After high school, my father and Scotty decided to stay close to home and attend the University of Akron. He [Haley] played all four sports there and won letters for each. He was a great athlete there. At Akron he was coached by Fred Sefton in football. He didn't talk too much about him, but he was glad to be associated with him.

While at Akron, he met my mother, Catharine. One day my mother was in the gym on campus when she saw my father, who happened to have his shirt off and nothing but a towel around his waist. She said he was the most handsome man she had ever seen. They started to date, but her family had a problem with them going out. They didn't approve of her dating a football player. I guess they didn't think too highly of the game back then—different from today. So her family sent her to Oberlin College to finish school. But that didn't stop them. They ended up getting married in 1924.

While at Akron, my father helped the team become very successful. In 1919 they only lost one game—to Wooster [Ohio] 19-0. It was Akron's best record up to that point. After his last college game against Case, the Akron Pros of the NFL tried to sign him to a contract so he could play in the big game against the Canton Bulldogs. But he suffered numerous injuries in the Case game and couldn't play.

In 1920 he did play professional football with the Canton Bulldogs, and there was a big article in the Canton paper announcing it. He was only five feet ten inches, and he ended up as Jim Thorpe's backup. In his first game, he carried the ball just a few times. He didn't play too much, but everybody seemed to talk about him the next day. During one of those few carries, a photographer shot him, and that photo was in the Canton newspaper.[2] It was the only football photo of the game, so everybody thought he must've had a good game. My son Tim has produced a photocopy of that photo. He's still trying to find an original.

As I said earlier, my father was Jim Thorpe's backup for a couple of games. I remember growing up, my father telling me about Thorpe. But being the girl in the family, I didn't pay too much attention to what he was saying. I know I am proud that my father played with someone like Jim Thorpe. My father used to get letters from Thorpe regularly after they stopped playing. Most of the letters would come around Christmas time. Thorpe would sometimes ask for money, and my father would send him some.

The era he played in, the pro game was considered a rough sport, and my father wasn't that big. He only weighed about 175 pounds. He always told the story about how he lost his two front teeth playing pro football. He seemed to be proud of that. Another story he told was how he lost most of his hair taking too many cold showers. He just enjoyed telling old football stories.

After playing for Canton, he went on to play a few games for the Dayton Triangles and the Akron Pros. In one game against the Columbus Panhandles, he played against four of the famous Nesser brothers. I think that was a thrill for him. We don't know actually how he got to play for Dayton. But he knew he wasn't going to play for very long. He mainly played pro ball on the weekend to help pay for the house he wanted. He ended up buying a colonial home for six thousand dollars.

After giving up football, my father became manager of the J. P. Loomis Company in Akron. It was a building supply company for the coal industry. He was happy to coach us in all the sports, especially my brother John. He never pushed us into athletics. He was more concerned with the sportsmanship of the game than the outcome. He believed in the saying, "It's not whether you win or lose, its how you play the game." He thought you had to be a good sport, and we thought that was great.

When I was born, we moved to Zanesville, Ohio, where my father was hired to work for the Pittsburgh Plate and Glass Company. But right when we got there, he suffered a stroke and passed away at the age of fifty-one. I am very proud of my father and what he accomplished. In the past couple of years, I've learned a lot about my father's football career. I think it's great that my family has had a connection to the growth of professional football.

Art Haley passed away on February 14, 1946, at the age of fifty-one in Zanesville, Ohio. His daughter, Ann Heslop, and her husband, Donald, now live in Akron. Their son, Tim Heslop, and his family live in Canton.

Extra Point

Nappy Nesser Picks up a Hobby

Al "Nappy" Nesser, one of the famous Nesser brothers, and Art Haley's former teammate with the 1923 Akron Pros, went on to play ten years in the NFL, the longest career in the NFL among all of the famous Nesser siblings. In 1927 he helped the New York Giants win their first-ever NFL championship. Al retired from the NFL in 1931 at the age of thirty-eight and went on to play several more seasons with a couple of semipro teams in Akron. But at the age of forty-five, he picked up a unique sporting hobby: boxing. I guess he missed the contact of professional football.

Walter Lingo

NFL Owner, 1922–1923 Oorang Indians

I believe my dad was an entrepreneur ahead of his time, perhaps like the
dot-com folks of today.
—Bob Lingo, son of former NFL owner Walter Lingo

*Bob Lingo, the son of Walter Lingo, was interviewed for forty-five min-
utes by the author in his hometown of LaRue, Ohio, on June 26, 2000.*

*Walter Lingo (1890–1966) was born in 1890 in LaRue, Ohio, a tiny
town of 800 people, north of Columbus. Lingo operated the Oorang
Dog Kennels in LaRue, where he developed a popular hunting breed, the
Oorang Airedale. In its heyday, Lingo's kennel sold thousands of
Airedales annually to customers including politicians, movie stars, and
sports celebrities. Lingo was also a showman and promoter who saw in
the fledgling National Football League an opportunity to showcase his
dogs before large crowds. For less than the cost of one of his Airedales,
Lingo bought an NFL franchise and in 1922 fielded the Oorang Indians.
Lingo's friend Jim Thorpe was player-coach, and the team's roster was
made up entirely of Native Americans, including top NFL talent such as
Pete Calac and Joe Guyon.*

*The Oorang Indians won only four games in two years (record of 4-16)
and folded after the 1923 season. Thorpe, Calac, and Guyon went on to
other NFL teams. Lingo's business failed like so many others during the
Great Depression. But Lingo's impact on the town of LaRue is still evident.
The community of LaRue holds a record that, it's safe to say, will never be
broken: smallest town to ever host an NFL franchise. And if such records
were kept, LaRue also would hold the record for the most unusual NFL
team: the 1922–1923 Oorang Indians.*

L ARUE, OHIO, WAS YOUR TYPICAL SMALL MIDWESTERN TOWN. WE HAD our restaurants and our youth hangouts. More young people worked on the farms, so we had less free time than the youth of today. We didn't have television, so we relied on more creativity as far as ice skating in the winter time, football, baseball, and activities of that nature in the summer and fall. It was a great little community. You could leave your door open—a different time than today.

My father, Walter Lingo, was not an athlete; he was an outdoorsman. He loved to be outdoors. He loved working with the dogs. I think that was one of the things that joined him with the Indians, the fact that they both loved the outdoor life. They liked working with animals. He was also a great fan of the old Wild West shows. That was the start of his ideas for halftime shows during the professional football games. He felt people needed something to do at halftime, so he came up with the idea to have halftime shows to help promote the dogs.

He started the dog business when he was about twelve or thirteen years old. He started on a very small scale with the hounds. Then he had a desire to raise a particular breed of dog, so he came up with the Airedale, the Oorang Airedale, which is different than the Airedale terrier because of his breeding. It has a stronger jaw, broader head. It was a more muscular dog. It was designed for hunting, especially big game hunting like bear, mountain lion, and so forth. It was a dog that required a lot of stamina in the field, not so much showmanship. At that time, nobody else was breeding that type of dog. It was a unique breed. He was very careful in the breeding of those dogs. He would only sell the most select dogs. He worked very hard to keep the breed pure.[1]

During the heyday of the kennel, when so many dogs were being shipped, my dad didn't breed the dogs at the kennel. He had a contract with several farmers to help. He didn't believe in raising the dogs in pens like they do today. He would take them and put them out on a farm. There they would have the pups, and he would select the pups he wanted and bring them back to the kennel for training. Depending on what their mission was going to be, the dogs would be trained for hunting, for show, or whatever. The Indians could sort of spot the more intelligent dogs. They helped put the right dogs in the right type of training.

I believe my dad was an entrepreneur ahead of his time, perhaps like the dot-com folks of today. He saw an opportunity to help his business, and professional football was just getting started, so he started the team. I'm not positive on the exact idea, but my dad had met Jim Thorpe before, and at that time Jim was looking for a business enterprise to get into. He [Thorpe] had his natural athletic abilities, which were at a premium at that time. So I think they just got their heads together and decided that Jim Thorpe was a great coach as well as an athlete, and he knew a lot of talented Indians from his Carlisle days that they could make a team. They just got together and thought they'd give it a try. In those days, that's what you did. You'd give it a try.

My father named the team after the dog business, the Oorang Indians. He paid one hundred dollars for the franchise. There's been some debate whether he actually paid the money or not, or whether he gave somebody a dog or something. The one hundred dollars was the going rate at that time for a franchise. My dad used to say he paid his players less than the average peanut vendor would make in an NFL game today.

Jim Thorpe and my father were very good friends—much more than business associates. Jim and his family would come back to LaRue and visit all the time, even after the team disbanded. Unfortunately, we lived in a rather small home, and they would have to sleep on the living room floor, which was alright to them because we would fix it up the best we could. They liked that. I remember my mother getting up at the crack of dawn to fix bacon and eggs. I never saw anybody who could eat so much bacon and eggs in my life. It was a very close relationship.

Thorpe would play football with us all the time. Somehow the local boys and my friends always seemed to know when he was visiting. We'd go out to the big field and play all day. He'd show us how to kick the ball. I think he enjoyed being around the boys, and we enjoyed being around him. One time I had a rather cheap child's football, and he kicked it pretty hard. It burst in half. I don't know whether he felt worse or I did. Anyhow, he replaced the ball.

The team would practice every day depending on the workload at the dog kennels. Football was a secondary mission for these players because they did everything at the dog kennel, from training the dogs to building the crates to ship the dogs in. They kept in good physical condition. That was more important than an actual practice. Some of the plays they ran were made up as they went. During the game, if they saw a weakness in the other team, they'd just make up a play and say, "Jim, I'm gonna go this way. Joe [Guyon], you go the other way, and I'll throw you the ball." More like sandlot football.

Since Thorpe was player-coach, I think it was difficult for him to organize everything. They didn't have anybody outside to probably criticize and spot weaknesses and so forth. That was a big factor. They also loved to hunt—coon hunting at night. So they played football in the day and went hunting all night. Their physical training got them in shape but wasn't up to speed as far as sleep was concerned. They really struggled in games, which is maybe why they didn't last very long.

My father gave it a try, and I know he was glad he attempted it. I think the timing was bad. That's when the Depression hit football. If it hadn't been for that, I think the NFL would've got a much earlier start. Like my dad, for instance, and many of the other early owners who were in debt, they borrowed money to keep it going. They didn't have the capital to survive the Depression. If that hadn't happened in the sequence it did, the NFL would have gotten off to a much quicker start.

After the team disbanded, my father went through a small depression. Naturally, when you lose all your money in the stock market crash, you go through a small depression. He was feeling pretty blue, and my mother was very inspirational in getting him back on his feet. He suddenly saw that there still was a place for a dog business. After the Depression, people got feeling better about themselves and the economy. He then got back into the dog business on a much smaller scale. Due to my mother's effort, he found out he had quite a list of previous dog owners. So they started mailing out catalogs, and it got back moving again—this time on a much smaller scale. He was happy with it.

My father moved on. He didn't watch much football after that. I think George Halas and Paul Brown used to invite him to various football functions and games, but he never attended them.[2] He'd always send a letter back with a thank-you note and so forth. He was more interested in what we were doing. He became a Boy Scout leader. We had the largest Boy Scout troop in the state of Ohio, right here in this little town. My dad was very interested in all kinds of youth activities. When I played football, the thing I remember most was that he never missed a game. To me, that was the most important thing in the world. That was more important than the NFL at that time. He was always there. He was a great dad.

To this day, my family gets letters talking about the Oorang Indians. But most of the letters are about the dog business. Surprisingly, most of them seem to think that the dog business is still thriving. I think everybody sort of wanted to cling to the past, from the letters I read. They didn't want to accept the fact it had gone. But I think it's important that we remember these places and the events that happened there.

My memories of the team are the fact that they were able to do as much as they did with as little as they had to do it with. The equipment was poor. The training facilities were poor. They were able to come together as men. They respected each other and played hard. They tried hard, and I think that's all you can ask of anybody. I'm proud of my father for his foresight and his willingness to take a chance and do something different.

Walter Lingo died in 1966 at the age of seventy-six. His son Bob is still living and makes his home in Delaware, Ohio. Today, a state of Ohio historical marker on Route 37 in LaRue recognizes Lingo's achievements and LaRue's distinction as the smallest town ever to host an NFL franchise. The marker was erected in 1997.

Extra Point

Thorpe Remembers the Oorang Indians

After retiring from the NFL, Thorpe recalled his fondest memory of the sport he made popular. "My professional football career reached its climax when I assembled the greatest Indian team of all time, the Oorang Indians, one of the finest group of professionals that ever played together."[3]

William Guthery, Sr.

End, 1922 LaRue (Ohio) High School

We didn't know the rules. We didn't really know how to handle the ball or how to catch it. Jim Thorpe and the Indians showed us how to do it.
—William Guthery, Sr.

William Guthery, Sr. (1905–) was interviewed by the author for forty minutes at his family home in LaRue, Ohio, on June 26, 2000. Guthery was born on September 20, 1905, and grew up on his family farm in LaRue. As a senior in 1922, he joined the town's first high school football team. That same year, Walter Lingo, owner of the Oorang Kennels and LaRue's leading businessman, brought Jim Thorpe and the Oorang Indians to town. The two teams practiced on the same field at the same time because the town had only one field suitable for football. Thus, Guthery and his teammates, who had never played organized football, had the benefits of coaching from National Football League veterans and future Hall of Famers such as Thorpe and Joe Guyon.

A T THE TURN OF THE TWENTIETH CENTURY, MY FAMILY STARTED A farm in tiny LaRue, Ohio, and when I was two years old, my father built the family home. That was the house I grew up in, and the family still owns it today. At that time, LaRue had six or seven groceries, four garages, and three automobile dealers. Now there's one grocery, no garages, and no automobile dealers. Times have changed. The town has never had more than 1,200 people. Today it is about 800. It's been around that number for a long time. The town is also divided by two railroad sections. Trains would stop in LaRue all the time. There were twenty-seven trains that would go through LaRue.

Growing up, I really didn't know much about professional football, let alone the NFL. It was just getting started in northeast Ohio and western Pennsylvania, which was the birthplace of pro football. When the Oorang Indians were organized in the early 1920s, the NFL wasn't more than three or four years old.

I can't remember when they announced that LaRue High School was fielding a football team; I just knew it was the thing to do. We had maybe fifteen or twenty guys out for that first team. We were very anxious to play. Everybody didn't have that privilege. I think some of the communities were a bit jealous of us because we had the only football team in the county. Of the nine schools in the county, we were the only one that had a football team.

As we were starting, the Oorang Indians became a household name around LaRue. For a while, Marion [Ohio] got credit for the Indians, but it was a fact that the dog kennel was in LaRue and the team was owned by LaRue resident Walter Lingo. I didn't know Lingo very well except that he was pretty successful. He owned a general store, a hardware store, a tire mill, and of course, the dog kennel, so they were pretty well established.

I think he had about twenty people working for him, and that was a lot of people in a little town like LaRue. All the dogs were shipped out from here—no trucks, just by train. You had several celebrities who would come in to pick up their dogs. I missed Jack Dempsey, but I do remember seeing Lou Gehrig and Charley Paddock. They would get off the train, and Lingo would have his picture taken with them for publicity.[1]

Both teams [LaRue High School and the Oorang Indians] started that year, and you can imagine what we were thinking because none of us had ever played football before. We didn't know the rules. We didn't really know how to handle the ball or how to catch a ball. Jim Thorpe and the Indians showed us how to do it. Our principal and coach, Mr. Morris, showed us a little, but he just explained it to us, where the Indians showed it to us. They showed us what to do. They showed us how to tackle, how to straight-arm, how to pass and kick. We did have one kid on the high school team, a husky fella. He had a temper. You'd tackle him or block him and he'd get up and hit you. He didn't last long. I think the Indians kind of enjoyed helping us out.

Thorpe was just a nice guy. He had his faults, but as a player he was impressive. He was very fast and in good condition. He had good coordination of his body and played clean. As I remember, there weren't any fouls or dirty play back then. It was just a clean sport. Maybe I didn't know any better. A lot of them played without headgear. I guess it was a pretty rough sport compared to today. I mean, your padding and your helmet and all that stuff didn't exist. No comparison.

Thorpe did have one policy and that was "always tackle." Don't just jump on a guy. I mean always get him off his feet when he is through running. Now, I only went to see one game, and that was played at nearby Marion since we didn't have a true football field. I think the Indians played the Columbus Panhandles, and at the beginning of the game, Thorpe would drop-kick. They didn't have placekickers in those days. He'd drop-kick from the 50-yard line one way and turn around and kick over the goal the other way. During the game I remember the team's offensive play. They would line up real quick before the other team got into position to start the next play. It worked sometimes.

But the team was more for Lingo to advertise his dog business and the Oorang Airedale. That was Lingo's idea—get the name out front. He was a great promoter. Once I was going to college in Cleveland, and a friend of mine says, "Hey, you're from LaRue, aren't you?" I said, "Yeah." He then shows me this picture in the [Cleveland] *Plain Dealer*. It had a photo of Lingo, Thorpe, and a bear. The caption read, "It's been a long time since there was a bear killed in Ohio." Well, Lingo always had a bear at the kennel to help train the hunting dogs, but the paper didn't know that. That's the kind of promotion he would do.

During the week, most of the Indians lived in town at a hotel called the Coon Pawn Inn. It was operated by a character who ran the *LaRue News*. There were a couple of them who lived there. They seemed to get along alright. Some of them drank, raised a little hell once in a while, but I don't remember any of them being put in jail or anything like that. One story I heard about was when the Indians were playing an exhibition game in Indianapolis. I guess three or four of them got in an argument with a taxi driver, and they laid the cab over on its side so the driver couldn't get out. They left him there.

The citizens of LaRue enjoyed them being there. Some of the Indians would work around town. Nick Lassa, whose Indian name was Chief Long Time Sleep, was the first one to arrive. The first time I saw him was east of New Bloomington. He was jogging to Marion. He was the first man I ever saw wearing shorts around here. He stayed around here until the early 1930s. The other ones kind of split up. Some of them went back to the reservation, while some stayed in Ohio. Pete Calac became a cop in Canton. Another one, Lo Boutwell, had a printing establishment over in Mechanicsburg, Ohio. They just kind of went their separate ways.[2]

Nick Lassa stood out the most because he was here for a long time. He was such a nice fella to have around. I remember going to a county fair with him, and they have these guys who ran the wrestling ring. They usually have an older wrestler with them. Well, Nick would wrestle this poor sap and win some money. Sometimes he'd win as much as fifty dollars.

I don't think the people of LaRue resented them being there because the Indians didn't really cause any trouble. Everybody was glad to see Lingo make a go of it because he was quite a success. But it was an oddity. I don't know if it helped the NFL, but everybody noticed it, which was good for LaRue. The Indians didn't play for much money or glory; they just had a hell of a good time doing it.

The town of LaRue still remembers the team, and with our community celebration every year called the "Oorang Bang," they will continue to remember. It was kind of dying out there, and everybody started to forget about them. But pro football has become so prevalent that it brought Jim Thorpe and the Oorang Indians back onto the scene again. It was something to get the people back together again. It was a good thing.

We appreciated the team. There probably wasn't any other town in the country that size that had a pro football team. You were proud to be from LaRue where the Oorang Indians were from.

William Guthery, Sr., lived on the family farm in LaRue until 1970, when he retired and moved to Ft. Pierce, Florida. His son continues to live at the family home in LaRue. Guthery is now ninety-nine years old and continues to follow the NFL every fall.

Extra Point

The 1923 Oorang Indians—Who Needs to Score?

The 1923 Oorang Indians were a very colorful team, yet a very bad team as well. The 1923 Indians finished with a record of 1-10, and were shut out five straight times during one stretch. During that five-game streak, the Indians were outscored 140-0, including a 57-0 defeat by the Buffalo All-Americans on October 21.

William Roy "Link" Lyman

Tackle, 1922–1923, 1925 Canton Bulldogs;
1924 Cleveland Bulldogs;
1925 Frankford Yellowjackets;
1926–1928, 1930–1931, 1933–1934
Chicago Bears

> We were the Canton Bulldogs. When we went to Chicago, we were al-
> ways the favorite. We had that much prestige.
>
> —Link Lyman

*William Roy "Link" Lyman (1898–1972) was interviewed twice at the
Pro Football Hall of Fame in 1964 and 1965. The Hall of Fame did these
interviews for a local Canton radio station. Both interviews were found
in the archives of the Pro Football Hall of Fame.*

*Lyman was born on November 30, 1898, in a small town in Ne-
braska aptly named Table Rock, where he grew up to be a rock-solid,
six-foot-two, 233-pound tackle. Lyman didn't play high school football
because there weren't enough boys to field a team; instead he went on to
the University of Nebraska and played four years of football from 1917
to 1921, sitting out the 1920 season.*

*After college Lyman signed on to play pro football, and in his first
three National Football League seasons, his teams went a combined 28-
1-4 and won three NFL titles (1922–1923 Canton Bulldogs and 1924
Cleveland Bulldogs). He won his fourth title with the 1933 Chicago
Bears. Very agile for his size, Lyman used shifting and sliding maneuvers
on defense to confuse his opponent's blocking assignments. This was the
beginning of modern defensive technique that would be used for many
years to come. Lyman played on only one losing team in fifteen years of
college and pro football. In 1964 he was inducted into the Pro Football
Hall of Fame.*

I WAS ALWAYS BIG FOR MY SIZE, BUT I DIDN'T START PLAYING ORGANIZED football until I got to college. You see, I was born in a small town called Table Rock, Nebraska, and we only had about six or seven boys in the whole school, so I couldn't play in high school. I did know a little about the game, but it wasn't until I reached the University of Nebraska in 1917 that I was able to actually play in a real game. From the first day, I just loved the game, and we had some pretty good teams, too. My senior year [1921], we only lost one game to Notre Dame, and we outscored our opponents 283 points to 17. That was a fun year.

After my senior year, I was contacted by Guy Chamberlin, who was an All-American at Nebraska a few years before me, and he wanted to know if I was interested in playing pro football. He was about to take charge of the Canton Bulldogs in the NFL, and he offered me a spot on the team, so I took it. I heard a lot about Chamberlin while at Nebraska. He was a hero there, so I thought playing for him would be great.

The pro league was just getting started when I joined the Bulldogs. It was organized in 1920 when they made Jim Thorpe the president. But Jim wasn't equipped properly to organize and handle the league situation, so the next year they hired Joe Carr—Joey Carr—who was a close personal friend of mine. I thought he did a great job of guiding the league through those pioneering days of pro football. Carr got some help from the likes of George Halas and Ralph Hay. They realized that they needed some regulations for this league to be successful. All of them worked hard at getting the league started.

When I joined the Bulldogs in 1922, we had a great team. We had such stars like Bird Carroll, Doc Elliott, Tex Grigg, Pete Henry, Duke Osborn, Harry Robb, and Dutch Speck. We were coached by Guy Chamberlin, and we didn't lose a game [10-0-2]. Chamberlin played, too. He was our best end. We had this play where he came around on an end-reverse, and sometimes he would get the ball on an end sweep, or we'd fake it to him and hand it to the fullback up the middle. Other times, our fullback Louie Smyth would drop back and hit me on a tackle-eligible play down the field. We would average a touchdown a game with Guy coming around from his end position. They couldn't stop it. While I was with the Canton Bulldogs, we won two NFL championships [1922–1923], and the city loved us.[1]

When I came to Canton, they had ninety-three diversified industries here. I've never seen a city that had that many diversified industries. It just goes without saying that had these men realized the magnitude of this game or what it was going to develop into, they would've never let this franchise get away. We were the Canton Bulldogs. When we went to Chicago, we were always the favorites. We had that much prestige.

We always filled the park in Chicago just because of the name Canton Bulldogs. The team was famous all over the world because of Jim Thorpe's association here in the earlier days—him and Joe Guyon and Pete Calac and that whole bunch—the Canton Bulldogs I would guess that sometime in the future, maybe not in my lifetime but sometime, I would predict that Canton will again have a team in the National Football League.

After the 1923 season, the city of Canton was having a hard time finding an owner who would keep the team in Canton. Finally, a man from Cleveland [Sam Deutsch] bought the franchise and moved the whole team there. So in 1924 we played as the Cleveland Bulldogs, and, led by our player-coach Guy Chamberlin, we won the NFL title for the third straight year. But we lost more money in Cleveland—about $30,000. So a group of us that included Rudy Comstock, Ben Jones, and myself got together, and we bought the Canton franchise back from Cleveland. We bought everything back for $3,500, and we played in 1925 as the Canton Bulldogs.[2]

Except for Guy Chamberlin and few others, we got the whole team back together, including Pete "Fats" Henry, the Hall of Fame tackle.[3] We had two fine days of sunshine for the first two Sundays, and we had good attendance—enough to pay the rest of the team but the three of us for the rest of the season. Then it started to rain on the third Sunday and every Sunday after that. It was mud and rain the whole time, and the three of us played for nothing the rest of the season. We played all right, but we were in the middle of the pack in the standings, so we were certainly disheartened at the end of the season.

At the end of the season, I got a call from George Halas of the Bears. He was about to go on a barnstorming tour with Red Grange, and he wanted me to play. The NFL president, Joe Carr, allowed Halas to bring a few more players on this tour, so I said yes. From that point on, I played for Halas. I ended up playing seven more seasons with the Bears.

Playing for the Bears definitely helped me get into the Hall of Fame, but it was Canton that I loved. When the Hall of Fame site was being considered, I was very much interested in doing anything I could to see that the Hall of Fame came to Canton. I don't think my family and I ever enjoyed a city as much as we did the city of Canton while I was playing there. I was very pleased to see George Halas and the other owners support the decision to put the Hall of Fame in Canton, and certainly the Canton Bulldogs carried a lot of prestige in helping the site to be located there.[4]

I was grateful to be elected into the Hall of Fame in 1964. I have great memories of the days I played in Canton, and no one can take those away from me. I appreciate it and was very thankful for the honor they gave me. The main thing it brought back was the memories of some very happy times spent with other great athletes. I also remember my speech, too, as William Umstattd of the Hall of Fame committee presented me.

Text of Link Lyman 1964 Hall of Fame Speech

Thank you Mr. Umstattd for that wonderful introduction. And may I salute the dignitaries here and all of you good people of the surrounding area and Canton and tell you what a wonderful event this has been to me. I have never seen such hospitality. I have never seen the likes of what is going on here now in Canton.

First, I would like to make a quick comparison here, that it really takes some doing to switch a western Nebraska cowpuncher into a steel man. But through the help of some able fellows like the Timken people and others here, we made the switch. And enjoyed the city of Canton and its people for about three years here and we have always remembered the happy events that went on here. Looking at this field, I am reminded of Meyers Lake, which is not too far from here, which consisted of just a solid hard, clay field. But on that field professional football history was made. And I just hope that some of the shadows, some of the things that went on, on that field here in Canton, that some of those great events in which Jim Thorpe, Joe Guyon, Ed Healey, George Trafton and hundreds of great All-Americans, where they made history and whom only a few have been honored as we are being honored today will eventually be honored over the years to come. That would by my wish today, if some of those things that happened over there could be transplanted to this great stadium here, and the memories of those great athletes who so admirably carried on in great fashion for pro football.

Myself, there are probably one or two hundred other fellows, that I would like to see receiving this honor today, but I guess their time will come. So let's simply close this by saying that this is a start of one of the nation's greatest events, as the future will prove. Because the parade, the event here, the Hall of Fame, whom you great people here in Canton have built, headed by the Timken group will certainly grow into something I think and truly believe if you folks have the vision and accept the challenge, that will compare with the Pasadena Rose Parade and the great Pasadena Carnival out there and the football game. It's yours to have if you want it. If you work hard enough it can be that big an event.

May god bless each and every one of you and please have that vision and keep making this a bigger and finer Canton for our Hall of Fame. Thank you very much.[5]

Winning those three championships with Canton [last one in Cleveland] has to be counted among the greatest thrills of my life. It's interesting to see the thinking of these athletes of today. The thing that thrills me today is to see my grandson Steve Kellogg, who's here with me this weekend. I've talked him away from athletics, except those athletics that he can take with him. He's studying architecture. He's getting his master's from Cal-Berkley. I pointed out to him that he should develop his golf game. He's a champion swimmer and he loves rugby, but participate in those sports that you can take with you into the business world. And above all, concentrate on those studies because without an education today, the average athlete is sunk. If they don't have the education, they certainly can't hold a position.

Link Lyman was a member of the second class ever to be enshrined at the Pro Football Hall of Fame in 1964. He coached seven seasons as line coach at his alma mater, Nebraska, before going into the insurance business in California. Lyman died of a stroke on December 28, 1972. He was seventy-four years old.

Extra Point

Playing with a Bunch of Hall of Famers

Over the course of his NFL career, Lyman was fortunate to play not only on some great teams but also with great players. While playing for four different teams, he played with eleven different Hall of Famers: Guy Chamberlin, Pete Henry, Paddy Driscoll, George Halas, Ed Healey, George Trafton, Red Grange, Bronko Nagurski, Bill Hewitt, George Musso, and Walt Kiesling.

Hal Broda

End, 1927 Cleveland Bulldogs

Looking back, there was quite a bit of civic pride about the Canton Bulldogs and pro football.

—Hal Broda

*Harold Broda (1905–1989) was interviewed at his home in Canton,
Ohio, on June 16, 1976. The twenty-minute interview was found in the
archives of NFL Films. Broda was born on July 27, 1905, in Canton,
Ohio, and grew up watching Jim Thorpe and the old Canton Bulldogs.
He played high school football at what is now powerhouse Canton
McKinley High School. After high school, Broda went on to captain the
first-ever undefeated team at Brown University in 1926. Broda's team
was nicknamed the "Iron Men" because all eleven starters played nearly
four full games without any substitutions.*

*After graduating, Broda turned down an offer to play with the then-
defending National Football League champion Frankford (Pennsylvania)
Yellowjackets, opting instead for law school at Case Western Reserve in
Cleveland. But the lure of the gridiron was too great, and he accepted an
offer to join the Cleveland Bulldogs for three games at the end of the 1927
NFL season. He retired from professional football after playing just those
three games. Broda remained a citizen of Canton until his death in 1989.*

I WAS BORN IN CANTON, OHIO, IN 1905, AND THE BIGGEST RIVALRY IN PRO
football was the Canton Bulldogs against the Massillon Tigers. Between those two local teams, our area saw a lot of great players.
Growing up in Canton, all of the boys were rather anxious to play football. I think we threw a football around more than we did a baseball as

young boys. Our heroes were the stars of the Canton Bulldogs professional team. Some of the adult population of Canton regarded pro football as a bum's life, but of course, to the young boys it seemed like a great life. We were able to see Jim Thorpe, Joe Guyon, Pete Calac, Link Lyman, Pete Henry, and a number of others. They were our heroes.

But the general opinion of pro football players at that time was considerably lower than it is now. Now they're regarded in a much higher category. Of course, at that time, a lot of those pro football players were college graduates, and a lot of them played under assumed names to protect themselves. So nobody actually knew who they were, but they would play. They would come into town the day before the game, practice with the team, then go out and play on Sunday, then leave town to go back to their respective homes or schools or wherever they were living.

I remember one time, Fritz Pollard, who was playing for the Akron team, told me that he would arrive in Akron on a Sunday morning, wind his way through town to the proper pool hall where the team met, then they would practice the plays in an open field next to the pool hall. Just before they would go out on the playing field, they would put their uniforms on and go out and start the game. But that wasn't anything unusual; most of the pro teams did that.

I loved going to the games on Sundays, but most of the time I had to make something up so my parents would let me go. My mother and father didn't want me to see any of the games on Sunday because it wasn't the "Godly" thing to do. So I'd say I was going out to play ball with the boys. Then we'd ride our bikes out to the game, lock them to a tree, and climb the fence. There we would watch the game without paying, which was pretty common with most boys at that time around Canton.

The player I loved to watch was Duke Osborn. He was your typical tough football player of that era—a scrappy player who played without a helmet. But they were all fun to watch. Not only were they great football players, they also were great to have around. They were always there to shake your hand or talk about the game, especially when I got older and was in high school. They would help coach us from time to time. See, our high school team would practice on the same field that the Canton Bulldogs would practice on. This was in the early 1920s, and the Bulldogs would be leaving the field. Their practice session would be over with when we would come out to start our practice. A number of the old pros would hang around and teach us the different facets of the game. Guy Chamberlin taught me some end play. Link Lyman and my favorite Bulldog, Duke Osborn, taught us some line play. Pete Henry taught me how to kick a football. They really helped us out.

I learned enough in high school that I got a chance to play college football at Brown University. I entered Brown as a freshman in the fall of 1923. I played for four years and had established somewhat of a reputation and regard as an All-American. I had some contacts from different pro teams to play with them after my graduation, but I had made arrangements to go to law school at Western Reserve in Cleveland. Therefore, I was not interested in playing pro football for any team that would take me away from my so-called law school studies, until I received a letter from the Frankford Athletic Association, the owners of the NFL's Frankford Yellowjackets outside of Philadelphia.

This letter said, "Dear Sir: At the present time we are planning another championship Yellowjacket football team. You are probably aware that we won the World Championship last year [1926]. We are taking the liberty to learn if you are interested in playing professional football next season, providing of course that your class graduates this June." I think there was somewhat of a gentleman's agreement between the pro league or pro owners to stay away from college football players until they'd graduated. That's probably why that sentence was put in there. "Our season would consist of twenty games, thirteen of which will be played on Saturday and seven games away on Sunday. The Association guarantees to pay the player his full salary regardless of injury or cancellation of games. It is our policy to have the team report at least two weeks before the opening game for a period of training with each player receiving thirty dollars per week for living expenses. If you are in position to play pro football next season, we would be glad to hear from you. As a matter of record, will you please advise us of your weight, height, and age. Trusting that we may have the pleasure of receiving a prompt reply. Very truly yours, Frankford Athletic Association." I was very much honored to receive a letter like this from the NFL champions, but I had made other arrangements that I could not get out of.

In that letter they ask, "As a matter of record, will you please advise us of your weight, height, and age." This is considerably different than what present football players run into, where they know all about the personal life, their speed, his method of having an esprit de corps spirit with the other teammates, which at that time pro football teams didn't bother too much about.

By then I had made arrangements to go to Western Reserve law school and also help coach football under Gordon Lock. I was to coach the ends and be head track coach. After having made these commitments, I couldn't play pro football. But that letter made me think about it. As our season was coming to an end in 1927, I was contacted by the

NFL's Cleveland Bulldogs to see if I wanted to play three games. This time I decided to play.

The Bulldogs were led by rookie quarterback Benny Friedman, who went on to make All-Pro that season.[1] They asked me to join them on a three-game road trip to be played in seven days. Many pro teams would do this—hire extra players at the end of the season to help fill out their roster, mainly because of injuries suffered during the season. So I was contracted to play these three games, and with the permission of the Athletic Administration at Western Reserve, I was going to play pro football. I received a salary of $300 for the first game and $250 for the other two games. I also got an expense account for meals of $3 a day, which at that time wasn't too bad.

We left for the East Coast with our first game against the Providence Steamrollers [November 20]. We beat them 22-0 at the Cyclodrome. The Cyclodrome was used primarily for motorcycle and bicycle races. It wasn't exactly an oval; it was probably more of a round saucer shape. Most of the fans sat high above the race track. There were very few seats down below the field. It was rather strange to play a game with all these boards alongside of you and fans being much higher.[2]

Four days later [November 24], we played in New York against Red Grange's New York Yankees. They had a good crowd, and we beat them, too [30-19]. After that game, we took a train to Chicago and played our third game in seven days with a contest against the Cardinals. We won our third game in a row [32-7]. We scored a lot of points with Friedman at quarterback. I think the Bulldogs led the NFL in scoring that year [209 points scored—tops in the NFL]. Even though I didn't contribute much in those three games, I did enjoy playing.

After those three games, I never played pro football again, mainly because of the fear of injury. If one player was injured, there was no provision made to pay for his injuries, his hospital bills, or provide an income for him while he may be laid up with that injury. So I gave up the sport. Also at that time, pro football wasn't an established profession to earn money. It was regarded as somewhat of a vagabond sport and a carefree life.

I went on to finish one year of law school at Western Reserve, then gave that up to go into the insurance business with my brother at a firm here in Canton. So I've stayed in Canton pretty much my whole life. Looking back, I think there was quite a bit of civic pride about the Bulldogs and pro football. There were some who didn't like it, but for the rest of us, we were glad they were there. But football has always been very popular in Canton.

Hal Broda died on February 13, 1989, in his hometown of Canton, Ohio. He was eighty-three years old. His NFL career consisted of just those three games with the 1927 Cleveland Bulldogs. In 2003 Brown University honored Broda by naming him to the school's All-Decade Team of the 1920s.

Extra Point

Friedman's High School Career

Broda's most famous teammate, Benny Friedman, was born on March 18, 1905, in Cleveland, Ohio. He began his football career by being cut as a sophomore from the East Tech High School team. Unfazed, he transferred to Glenville High, and as a senior he led his school to the Cleveland city football championship. He concluded his high school experience as the senior class president and was chosen to deliver the commencement address at graduation. In 1979 Friedman developed a blood clot in his left leg and had it amputated. In constant pain, he committed suicide on November 23, 1982. In a note to his family, he explained that he didn't want to finish life as "the old man on the park bench." But on February 5, 2005, Friedman's legacy was honored with the highest achievement, by being elected to the Pro Football Hall of Fame with Fritz Pollard, Dan Marino, and Steve Young.[3]

Glenn Presnell

Tailback, 1928–1930 Ironton Tanks,
1931–1933 Portsmouth Spartans,
1934–1936 Detroit Lions

> We'd put on our shoes and sweatshirts and practice in this open field.
> We'd get back on the bus after the workout smelling like a bunch of
> goats. Those were great days.
>
> —Glenn Presnell

*Glenn Presnell (1905–2004) was interviewed by the author for an hour
on February 21, 1999, at his home in Ironton, Ohio. Presnell was born
in Gilead, Nebraska, on July 28, 1905, and overcame the tragedy of his
father's death to earn All-American honors at the University of Nebraska. After graduating, he declined several offers from National Football League teams to sign in 1928 with the semipro Ironton Tanks. Ironton's offer included not only a competitive salary, but also a job teaching
science in the Ironton schools.*

*After three successful years in Ironton, Presnell moved on to play
for the Portsmouth Spartans of the NFL. After making All-Pro in
1933, Presnell decided to retire, mainly because the Spartans were sold
to G. A. Richards, a Detroit businessman, who moved the team to the
Motor City and renamed them the Detroit Lions. After hearing an offer he couldn't refuse from the Lions management, Presnell returned to
the NFL and played three more seasons with the Lions, helping them
win the 1935 NFL championship. He retired after the 1936 season and
began a long college coaching career that included ten years as head
football coach at Eastern Kentucky University (1954–1963). Presnell
also served as the university's first full-time athletic director from 1963
until his retirement in 1971.*

I WAS BORN IN GILEAD, NEBRASKA, AND MY FAMILY MOVED AROUND several times when I was growing up. My father was a foreman on the railroad, so he was transferred a lot. We lived in Kansas for a while and then Calhan, Colorado, where I graduated from junior high school. Then, before I started high school, we moved to DeWitt, Nebraska, and that's where I saw my first football game. I was a fourteen-year-old freshman. DeWitt had a very good football team at that time, so the following year I decided to go out for the team.

My sophomore year at DeWitt was very tough. My father was killed in town, so I wanted to quit school and help out my family. But my mother didn't want me to. She wanted me to stay in DeWitt and finish school. So my mother moved away to stay with her folks, and I ended up staying at a friend of the family's who had a dairy farm. I would get up to work on the farm in the morning, then go to school, and come back and finish working on the farm. That kept me busy for a couple of years. I played three years of high school football. We didn't have a true coach. Our coach was a local dentist in town who had played football at Creighton University. He was a good coach, and we had some successful teams in DeWitt.

I had a pretty good career in high school, so several of my friends from DeWitt who were attending the University of Nebraska encouraged me to enroll. They belonged to a fraternity in Lincoln, so they gave me a job waiting tables at the frat house because they knew I didn't have much money except what I earned in the summertime. So I waited tables at the frat house, and as a sophomore, I went out for the football team. Fortunately, I made it.

I played three varsity seasons at Nebraska, and as a sophomore [1925], we played Illinois with the great Red Grange. That was Grange's senior season. He had that tremendous junior year when he scored all those touchdowns. But that day, we bottled him up pretty good. We had an All-American tackle by the name of Ed Weir, and he was in the Illinois backfield all afternoon. I also played against Ken Strong in college. He's now in the Pro Football Hall of Fame. We played New York University, where Ken was known for his running ability and his punting. So our coach said, "Now you better play deep enough because that guy Strong can kick that ball a mile." I can remember the first time he punted. I got back and he kicked the ball over my head. It went out of bounds at about our own 15-yard line. So, on the next play I tried to redeem myself, and I took the ball and ran it all the way back for a touchdown. It was one of the longest runs I ever made in college.[1]

My senior year [1927] I led the nation in yards gained and made several All-American teams. Because of my play, I received several offers to play professional football. I had offers from the Providence Steamrollers, Kansas City Cowboys, and the New York Giants. All those teams were in the NFL at that time. But it was an offer from the Ironton Tanks in Ironton, Ohio, that intrigued me the most. A man by the name of Nick McMahon made me a contract offer that was the same as the NFL teams, but he also offered me a teaching job with the Ironton school system. That appealed to me because I figured if I couldn't play pro football or if I got hurt, I'd still have my teaching job to fall back on. So I decided to sign with the Ironton Tanks [1928].[2]

I didn't know too much about professional football at that time, just from what I read in the newspapers. It wasn't as publicized as it is today. Most of the players on the Tanks were college graduates, and they too taught in the school system. That's how the Tanks operated. They would get college graduates to come to town to play and give them jobs teaching. We played teams out of Columbus, Cincinnati, and Akron, teams from Pennsylvania and Kentucky. But our biggest rival was the team from Portsmouth, a town just twenty minutes away from Ironton. We had fans from both towns come out for those games because they were so close to one another. There was a lot of betting with the Portsmouth games. That was one of the things that went on—a lot of gambling in those days.

Earle "Greasy" Neale was our coach in Ironton, and he was an exceptional coach. That's why he is in the Hall of Fame. He was an innovator with the Tanks. He started looping his lineman, which was a new innovation at that time but quite common now. Instead of charging straight ahead, Neale had us looping around to try and fool the blockers on offense. I remember playing Portsmouth in 1930, and they had a strong running game with Willis [Bill] Glassgow from Iowa, Chief McLain and Chuck Bennett from Indiana. They had some good football players for Portsmouth, but we looped our lineman and beat them.[3]

We had several good years in Ironton, especially in 1930 when we beat three NFL teams. We played the New York Giants in Cincinnati and we were losing 12-6. At the end of the game, we forced them to punt, and I ran the ball out of bounds to stop the clock. I asked the timekeeper how much time was left. In those days, they kept the time on the field with a watch. The official looked at his watch and said, "You have three seconds to play." So there was only one thing to do and that was to try a long pass. We were at about midfield, so I took the snap from center and started to one side, then I got loose and went to the other side of the field. Everybody was chasing me, and I see our little halfback, Gene Alford, in the end zone waving his hands frantically, so I threw him the ball for the touchdown.[4] We kicked the extra point and won 13-12. That was quite a farewell finish to a football game.

A couple of weeks later, we played the Chicago Bears in Cincinnati, and we beat them 28-14. I had a pretty good day against them. One play I remember was an 88-yard touchdown run. You see, I had sprained my ankle the week before, and prior to the game, Greasy Neale taped it up real tight so I could play. I broke loose off tackle, dodged Red Grange, and went 88 yards for the touchdown. It was quite a thrill for us to beat teams from the National Football League. That was quite an accomplishment in those days.

We had a solid team in Ironton in 1930. We had good players at all positions. We didn't have as many players as some of the other teams did. I think we had about eighteen men on our squad in those days. The Depression hit Ironton at that time, and a lot of people were out of work. In Ironton, they just decided they couldn't afford to support the team anymore, which they couldn't. So the Tanks folded.

I decided to take a high school coaching job across the river in Russell, Kentucky. I was just going to stay there and coach at the high school until the Portsmouth Spartans, who had just joined the NFL, wanted me to play for them. Since I only played the three years in Ironton, I thought I had some good years left in me, so I signed with the Spartans.[5]

I signed with the Spartans in 1931 for $4,200 a season. That wouldn't be one game today, but that was quite a bit of money back in those days. I joined the Spartans right at the same time they hired Potsy Clark as their head coach. We called Potsy "the Little General" because he was a strict disciplinarian. He worked us real hard. He was a stickler for conditioning. I think we were always in better shape than most of the teams we played. Potsy wouldn't stand for any horseplay. He just wouldn't take any lip from anybody. He would teach just straight-up football. He was an exceptional coach.[6]

Potsy had his moments. We didn't travel by train much in those days; it was mainly by Greyhound bus. Some of our road trips east would be pretty long, and we wouldn't have a chance to work out, so Potsy told us to pack a pair of shoes and a sweatshirt on the bus with us. We'd be going along sometime in the middle of the afternoon, and he'd see this open field, so he'd have the driver stop the bus. We'd put on our shoes and sweatshirts and practice in this open field. We'd get back on the bus after the workout smelling like a bunch of goats. Those were great days.

Portsmouth fans were very enthusiastic about their team. Practically as many fans came out to watch us practice as would come out for the games. They were very loyal also. They would go out of their way to entertain the players. They would invite the players into their homes for meals—we were their team—which they didn't do in Detroit when we moved there. We just lived by ourselves and never got acquainted with any townspeople. We got well acquainted with the people of Portsmouth. Everybody who knew you would come out to the games or at least to watch practice. In Detroit, nobody paid much attention to you.

The Spartans had some pretty good players when I played there, and we didn't like to lose. Many of the Spartans made All-Pro, including Dutch Clark. Now, Clark was a very shifty runner. He was an average passer but an exceptional dropkicker, which is a lost art today. He was very well liked by all the players. He had a wonderful personality. We were very good friends, even though we were competing a lot of times for the same position.[7]

Another good friend of mine was Ox Emerson. Ox wasn't very big for a professional guard—about 190 pounds—but he was so quick and agile that he made a lot of tackles. He was hard to block. He was just a perfect gentleman. We used to call him the "Southern Gentleman Number One" because he was such a nice guy. We kept in touch all these years until he passed away [1998]. We'd call each other about once a month. He used to call me the Blonde Blizzard. He'd always say, "Come on Blizzard, let's go" with his real southern accent.

Another good player we had was Father Lumpkin. He'd play without a helmet until they started to enforce the rule where you had to wear one. He always said the helmet made him dizzy. Besides the helmet, Lumpkin wouldn't wear socks, either. See, we had to pay for our own socks, and to save money, he'd just play with no socks. He was a great blocker. He was about six feet two inches, weighed about 210 pounds, and he was a really tough, hard-nosed football player.[8]

It was amazing to see a town the size of Portsmouth have an NFL team and a stadium like they had. The only other city in the country that could compare was Green Bay. Portsmouth had a bitter rivalry with the Packers at that time because of the small-town connection. We almost won the league title from Green Bay in 1931, but the Packers edged us out when they canceled a game scheduled for Portsmouth late in the season when we were one game behind them. The league then awarded the Packers the championship, and this made Potsy Clark angry. He told us when the Packers visit Portsmouth next season that we would beat them with just eleven men. Before the game in 1932, he gave us a pep talk by saying, "Now you eleven men that are starting, you're going to stay out there. The only way you're going to come out of this game is to be carried off on a stretcher." So we played the entire sixty minutes with eleven players and won the game 19-0. In Portsmouth it was called the "Iron Man Game."

By winning that game, it helped us tie the Chicago Bears for first place in the NFL standings. Because there wasn't a championship game, George Halas of the Bears and Harry Snyder of Portsmouth got together and agreed to have a one-game playoff game. That was the first-ever playoff game in NFL history. Joe Carr of the league office approved the idea, and the game was scheduled to be played in Chicago on December 18. But because it was played after the regular season, we lost Dutch Clark, who had to go back to Colorado College to coach basketball. The school wouldn't let him play.[9]

Then, when we got to Chicago to play the game, the city had a tremendous snowstorm and Wrigley Field was unplayable. So Halas and Snyder agreed to play the game at Chicago Stadium, where there had been a circus the week before. The stadium didn't smell very good, but it did have dirt on the field so we could play.

The game was played indoors under restricted conditions. The field was 80 yards long. They eliminated field goals, and we moved the ball in from the sidelines, which was a board fence used for the hockey games. The ball was placed 5 yards from the sidelines, like a hash mark today. That was the start of hash marks used in professional football, which we didn't have at that time.

It was an unusual environment to play a football game, and the footing was very treacherous. My favorite play was an off-tackle dive. Once, we were down near the goal line and I was going off right tackle. As I planted my foot, it skidded out from under me, and I went down. There was a big hole, and I would've easily scored to give us the lead.

The game was a scoreless battle till the very end, when the Bears had the ball at our goal line. We stopped Bronko Nagurski three times. Then on fourth down, they called a forward pass. Nagurski took the ball, started to plunge in the line, then jumped up in the air and threw a flip pass to Red Grange in the end zone.[10] We were sure that he was going to run the ball because he wasn't anywhere near 5 yards back of the line of scrimmage, which was the rule in those days. You had to be 5 yards back before you could throw a forward pass. It was an illegal pass, but they counted it anyway. They kicked the extra point, and late in the game, our center snapped the ball over our punter for a safety, and they won 9-0. It was an interesting game.

The following year, I assumed Dutch Clark's role when Dutch decided not to come back to the Spartans. I had a real good season. I led the league in scoring and made All-Pro. I also played eight straight games for sixty minutes. I would've played some more except I hurt my shoulder against the Giants. That was the way it was in those days. You didn't have a lot of substitutions. You just stayed in there and played.

The rest of the year was a tough one for Portsmouth. We didn't get paid for the last three or four games. We had a team meeting and decided: What do we got to lose? We might as well go ahead and play. We thought if we continued to play, then somehow we'd get paid. But most of us didn't—at least I didn't. The team lost over twelve thousand dollars that season and had to do something about the franchise. Harry Snyder got an offer from Mr. G. A. Richards, who bought the team and moved them to Detroit.[11]

By this time, I had accepted a coaching job at the University of West Virginia. I was there for spring ball when Mr. Richards wouldn't leave me alone. He called me and couldn't understand why, after leading the league in scoring and making All-Pro, I wanted to retire. So he made me an attractive offer by almost doubling what I was making at West Virginia. So I went to Detroit and played three more seasons.

That first year in Detroit [1934], we had a real good defensive team. Of course, we wouldn't stand up today with the forward passing as it is. Most of the teams in my day ran the ball. We shut out the first seven opponents that year until we gave up a touchdown against Pittsburgh. We still won that game 40-7. We had a real good team that season, but we lost our last three games to finish in second place. In 1935 we went on to win the Western Division and beat the Giants 26-7 to win the NFL championship.[12] That was the high point of my professional career. Potsy talked me into playing one more season. And I thought playing nine years of pro ball was enough, so I finally retired after the 1936 season.

Several people have brought my name up for the Hall of Fame, but I'm not in there. I'd like to be in, but for some reason I've slipped through the cracks. I have as good statistics as some of the people that are in there now. But I don't resent it at all. They do a good job with the Hall of Fame selections.

After I retired from coaching, I moved back to Ironton, Ohio, with my wife Mary. I always thought of this area as my hometown, so we built a home here in 1975, and we live on a street named Happy Hollow. It was a lot of fun playing in Portsmouth. It was much different than playing in a big city like Detroit. I remembering going down to the Elks Club here in Portsmouth. We would practice in the morning, then go to the Elks Club and play cards in the evenings. They were very kind to us in Portsmouth.

It was interesting to play in a small town, especially Portsmouth. They remember the team and the players after all these years. I just feel lucky to be the last one left. It's fun to reminisce and look back on all those great days. They'll always be proud of the fact that they had a National Football League team there at one time. Think about it— Portsmouth, Ohio, in the NFL.

I do follow the game today. I'm a great college football fan. I love to watch the college games on Saturday. It's changed quite a bit. They pass a lot more than we did. When I played, if we threw seven or eight passes in one game, it was a wide-open game. Now they throw on every play.

That's how it has changed. We played a strictly running game. If you had Bronko Nagurski on your team, wouldn't you run the ball? He was so hard to tackle because right when you went to tackle him, he would lower his arm and block you off. He was that strong, and he was also one of the fastest of the Bears' players.

Our equipment was nothing like today. Ours was made out of leather, which made the equipment much heavier. By the time you got on the heavy shoulder pads, the heavy hip pads, and other pads, you felt like you gained thirty pounds. I was fortunate. I was never really injured like some of the players from my era. I remember our helmets didn't have any facemasks back in those days, and if a guy got hit in the face, he would lose some teeth or maybe got his nose broken. That happened to several of my teammates at different times, but I was lucky. I must have been a good dodger because I was never really hit hard in the face. But I enjoyed it.

It was a challenge to me to see whether I could make it in pro football or not. I enjoyed my nine seasons of pro ball very much and made a good living while doing it. I'd just like to be remembered as a good football player. That's all.

In a six-year NFL career, Glenn Presnell led the league in scoring once (1933), was selected first- or second-team All-Pro four times (1931–1934), and in 1934 kicked a 54-yard field goal against the Green Bay Packers (October 7) that stood as an NFL record for nineteen years and as a Lions team record for sixty-one years, when Jason Hanson kicked a 56-yarder against the Cleveland Browns on October 8, 1995.

On July 24, 2004, just four days before Presnell's ninety-ninth birthday, Ironton honored him with a Glenn Presnell Day and presented him with a key to the city. Seven weeks later, on September 13, 2004, Glenn Presnell died at the age of ninety-nine. He was the last surviving member of the Portsmouth Spartans.

Extra Point

Home Field Advantage

No other teams in the NFL during the early 1930s had a greater home field advantage than the Portsmouth Spartans and the Green Bay Packers. From 1930 through 1933, the two small-town teams combined for a record of 41-4-6 at home (the Packers were 22-2-2, and the Spartans were 19-2-4). The Packers still hold the NFL record for the most consecutive home games without a defeat—30 (27 wins and 3 ties)—set during 1928 to 1933.

Dr. Louis Chaboudy

Portsmouth Spartans Fan,
1930–1933 Portsmouth Spartans

I'm sure I was just like many other young kids in Portsmouth that felt the Spartans were certainly our heroes.

—Dr. Louis Chaboudy

Dr. Louis Chaboudy (1919–2003) was interviewed by the author for forty-five minutes at his home in Portsmouth, Ohio, on July 1, 2000. Chaboudy was born in Portsmouth in 1919, a year before the National Football League was founded. He was a teenager when the Spartans played in Portsmouth from 1930 to 1933. Like many boys in the city, he idolized the players, hung their pictures on his bedroom wall, and was heartbroken when the team moved to Detroit after the 1933 season.

But Dr. Chaboudy never ceased being a Spartans fan and never ceased championing the team and its players. He campaigned for Glenn Presnell's induction into the Pro Football Hall of Fame, and he helped organize the 1970 reunion of former Spartans players in Portsmouth. He also initiated a successful effort to have the city's stadium renamed Spartan Stadium.

IN THE 1920S, PORTSMOUTH, OHIO, WAS A REAL INDUSTRIAL CITY. WE had the shoe industry, which was very prevalent in this area. There was a time when we had four active shoe factories going at once, the biggest being the Selby Shoe Company, which helped put up some of the money to bring the Portsmouth Spartans into the NFL. At that time, Portsmouth was considered the industrial center between Cincinnati and Pittsburgh along the Ohio River. It was quite exciting.

When the Portsmouth Spartans joined the National Football League in 1930, I was in junior high, and when they finished their last season in 1933, I was a sophomore in high school. Throughout that time, I knew everything about them. I was always interested in sports, and I ended up playing football my last two years in high school. At that time, the influence of the Spartans was tremendous as far as the high schools were concerned in this area. They were very popular.

The Spartans created a great feeling of pride throughout the community when they played here because most everyone knew something about the NFL. That's just about the only thing anybody talked about was the Spartans: what they were doing, where they were playing, the results, and so forth. It was quite an honor to be in the NFL from a town of this size. And not only that, but they gave a very good account of themselves. They were a very successful team. Their first season they had a losing record [5-6-3], but the last three years, they were either at or near the top in the standings.[1]

Going to a Spartans game was a very thrilling event. They played most of their games on Sunday afternoon, until night football came along. During those days, you could just about count on most of the sports fans being at the Spartans games. Sometimes we would climb the fence to get in, but other times my father would take me. He used to always pay for his ticket, but when we would go through the gate, he'd just shove me right ahead of him. I was little and he could get away with it. That's how it worked. As far as the actual ticket price, I think it was around two dollars.

A typical Spartans fan was very vocal. I don't like to relate to these types of things, but I do remember some betting at games. Some of the games I attended, if you were sitting up in the top section of the stands or the bleachers, you might see a fella down six or seven rows wanting to make a bet. He might want to bet on who scores next or whatever. He'd just stand up and wave that dollar bill in the air. Sure enough, there'd be somebody to take him up on it. That was the extent of the gambling.

They also had a PA system at the game, and we had an announcer, L. T. Henderson, who was very good. He would give you a resume of where the Spartans players had gone to college and so on. Then, of course, we had a very popular player by the name of Father Lumpkin. He had played his college ball at Georgia Tech, so whenever he'd make a play or be introduced at the beginning of the game, they'd always play the song "Rambling Wreck from Georgia Tech" over the PA system. There was a lot of enthusiasm at the games.

I'm sure I was just like many other young kids in Portsmouth that felt the Spartans were certainly our heroes because in those days, you either played football or watched it. I had pictures of all the Spartans on the wall of my bedroom. They're gone now, but I really prized those photos as a youth. They were my heroes. In those days, it wasn't a matter of getting autographs as much as it was having a chance to meet the players and shake their hands. My father used to take me down to the old smoke house on the corner of Fifth Street, where after the game, win or lose, some of the Spartans would come down and give people a chance to shake their hands and congratulate them and so forth.

The most famous player during those years was Dutch Clark. He was a triple-threat player: he could pass, he was an excellent runner, and he could drop-kick. He's the only Spartan inducted into the Pro Football Hall of Fame. It's been about ten or twelve years, but we started a campaign to get Glenn Presnell inducted. We just couldn't get it done. I still think he belongs there because he was an excellent football player and a very good open-field runner. He played both offense and defense as well as anybody from that era.

The interesting thing about Presnell was that he played three years with the Ironton Tanks, who were a really good semipro team around here. Although they weren't in the NFL, they played a lot of the NFL teams and beat the likes of the New York Giants and Chicago Bears. I think that has hurt Presnell [not getting into the Hall of Fame], playing only six NFL seasons, because he certainly belongs there.

Another fella we had was Ernie Caddell. He was an All-American at Stanford University. He was absolutely an excellent runner—very fast. At guard was Ox Emerson. They used to call him the "Watch-Charm Guard." He was a great defensive player. He wasn't that big. He only weighed about 190 pounds. I was fortunate enough to get to see him down at his home in Austin, Texas, before he passed away.[2]

Probably our most popular player was Father Lumpkin, who we called "Pop." He was one of the toughest human beings I ever saw. I remember seeing him wrestle during the off-season. He was just a very athletic individual. He was a great blocker, and he would say if he didn't take out two men on each play, then he wasn't doing his job. He meant putting them on the ground, not just bump them and go ahead.

Most of the Spartan players were in some way mentioned on an All-American team. They had a lot of talent. The fellas on the team had great respect and regard for each other. They stayed together because they didn't make much money. It was just a spirit of cohesiveness which came from playing in a small town. They really carried it out in the games.

The most famous game played in Portsmouth was between the Spartans and the Green Bay Packers in 1932. This came from the fact that the previous year, Green Bay was declared the champion of the league on paper. At that time, there wasn't a championship game, and as the season was coming to a close, it was evident that the Spartans and the Packers might tie for the title. They were supposed to play a game against each other in Portsmouth late in the season. It had been agreed verbally at the start of the year.

This is where the Spartans made a big mistake because they didn't get it in writing. So, when it became evident that the Spartans could tie for the championship if they won the game, the Packers then backed out. The Spartans management made an appeal to Joe Carr, who was president of the NFL, but he awarded the championship to Green Bay, since there wasn't any written proof.[3]

That really incensed Spartans coach Potsy Clark, who went to the Portsmouth paper and declared that when Green Bay visits Portsmouth the following season the Spartans would not only beat them, but they wouldn't use one substitute. That's exactly what happened. Portsmouth beat Green Bay 19-0 without making one substitute. It was called the "Iron Man Game." The town is very proud of that game.

In 1994 the city dedicated a mural to that game as well as honoring the team. It sits along the floodwall in downtown Portsmouth with the other murals that represent the history of the town. On the mural is a picture of Glenn Presnell scoring one of the touchdowns in the Packers game. The original photo appeared in the *Columbus Dispatch*. It was on the front of the sports page. At the bottom of the mural, we put a simple sentence to honor the team: "Gone but Not Forgotten."

I was crushed to hear that the Spartans were leaving, as a lot of the younger people were. I was just beginning to play football myself at that time, so it just broke my heart. We really enjoyed seeing them play. It was a real treat to go down to the stadium, not only to see our Spartans play, but to see all the big stars of the National Football League. We saw Red Grange, Benny Friedman, and Ken Strong. We saw Shipwreck Kelly, Cal Hubbard, and Johnny Blood. Nowadays, when you hear these names mentioned on the television and they say so-and-so is a Hall of Famer, well I've seen most of those fellas play right here in Portsmouth. It was really a treat to see them.[4]

A man from the radio business named [George A.] Richards bought the team from Portsmouth and moved it to Detroit. I've heard several stories about the amount that was paid for the team. I think it was around fifteen thousand dollars, if you can imagine that. It just doesn't seem possible. That's the way it was back then.

It's been about seventy years since they left here, and the reaction I get when I travel out of town is just amazing. The respect that people have for the old Spartans in various cities is just great. An example of that happened a while ago when I was visiting Chicago, and I heard that they had a huge picture of the 1932 indoor game between the Spartans and the Chicago Bears. That was the first play-off game in NFL history. Well, I heard there was a picture of that game hanging up in old Chicago Stadium where the Bulls and Blackhawks used to play. So I went over there to see this picture, and I saw an older gentleman with gray hair who was taking tickets. I told him that I was from Portsmouth, Ohio, and he just lit up like a Christmas tree. He said, "Oh, you know about the Spartans." I said, "Yeah. In fact, the reason I came here was to see that picture I've heard about." So he personally escorted me clear to the other side of the stadium to show me this picture.

In 1970 we had a reunion for the old Spartans in Portsmouth. It was the first time ever that they had been back as a team. My friend Jim Secrist and I were very much involved in getting that event done. We made arrangements to get them all back to Portsmouth. It was a lot of work to do all the mailings and everything. One of the reasons we were able to pull it off was the fact that the Detroit Lions, who have a reunion almost every five years, were having one the same year, so we had a good chance of getting a fair number of former Spartans to come down here. That's the way it worked out. The reunion was held in early August, and we had a total of nine of them return. Of course, we had Cyrus Kahl. He was living here in Portsmouth. And we had Ox Emerson, Glenn Presnell, and Father Lumpkin all come back.[5]

It was just an absolute wonderful reunion. They were so glad to see each other. It was really fun to listen to their stories of the team. I can remember Father Lumpkin when we escorted him down to the American Legion hall from the Holiday Inn. He got the biggest kick out of the various things along the way, going through downtown and seeing Gallia Street. They were all very appreciative of us having done this for them. At that time, we had invited all the Spartans back, including Potsy Clark, who was still living at that time. Jim Secrist and I had a three-way phone conversation with Potsy from his home in Thousand Oaks, California. He couldn't get over the fact that we were doing this. His health prevented him from coming. He couldn't understand why there weren't more Spartans in the Hall of Fame. He mentioned Glenn Presnell and George Christensen.[6] It was a real thrill to talk to him. He certainly had fond memories of Portsmouth when he was here.

As part of the Spartans' reunion, we had the football stadium renamed Spartan Stadium in honor of the team. I'm very proud of that because I sort of got that idea rolling. We had to pass it through City Council and everything, but they were very cooperative, and we got it changed. That stadium just absolutely flares up all my memories of those days and that team. For a town this size, I don't know where you'd find another one that compares with it.[7]

Thinking of the Spartans has never ceased being a very rewarding type of memory for me. Think about it: Whenever you would go anyplace in the country and you talked to somebody that's a little older and you mention the Portsmouth Spartans, they just immediately have a very good account of them. I just think it's one of the few things that we have in this community that can really exemplify the good because they really represented the town well.

Dr. Louis Chaboudy practiced medicine in Portsmouth for more than forty years before his death at age eighty-four on November 11, 2003. His widow, Ava, continues to live in Portsmouth.

Extra Point

Wednesday Night Football in Portsmouth, Ohio

On September 24, 1930, the Portsmouth Spartans hosted the Brooklyn Dodgers in one of the NFL's earliest night games. Universal Stadium housed over 6,000 fans as the hometown Spartans defeated the Dodgers 12-0. The following morning, the *Portsmouth Times* said, "Night football is here to stay, at least in Portsmouth." The Spartans went on to have eight more Wednesday night football games in 1931 and 1932. Nearly forty years before Monday Night Football started on ABC, Portsmouth had Wednesday Night Football.[8]

Leo Blackburn

Portsmouth Spartans Fan,
1930–1933 Portsmouth Spartans

The Portsmouth Spartans were the high point athletically for our city. We'll never exceed that, and because it is a high point, I think they will always be remembered.

—Leo Blackburn

Leo Blackburn (1911–2001) was interviewed by the author for forty minutes on July 1, 2000, at his home in Portsmouth, Ohio. Leo was born in Portsmouth on August 1, 1911, and grew up playing football with his older brothers. One of his brothers, Tom Blackburn, played quarterback for Wilmington College and went on to lead Dayton University to national success as head basketball coach (1947–1964). Leo was too light to play college football but became a fan of the Portsmouth Spartans when the team joined the National Football League in 1930.

Leo attended many Spartan games and wrote a poem about the team that was published by the Portsmouth Times *in 1997. He later went on to become a local historian for Portsmouth, writing several books and articles about the small town.*

I GOT INTERESTED IN FOOTBALL BECAUSE OF MY OLDER BROTHERS, ESPECIALLY my brother Tom. We used to practice kicking and passing and so forth. They told me all about the sport. I used to play a lot of sandlot football while growing up. Since I was very light, I didn't see myself playing past high school, but I loved the sport. My brother Tom went on to Wilmington [Ohio] College and played quarterback for three years. He then went on to become the head basketball coach at Dayton

University, where he put that team on the map. I followed Tom to Wilmington, but I only weighed 116 pounds, so I was cut from the football team my sophomore year.

I got interested in the Portsmouth Spartans from the very start. In fact, I was a sophomore in high school when Jim Thorpe played here for the Portsmouth semipro team. I'd always heard about him being such a great athlete. Seeing him here got me interested even more.[1] I can remember the great rivalry between the Portsmouth teams and the Ironton teams. Those were excellent games. In 1930 those two teams played their last game between themselves, and the star was Ironton halfback Glenn Presnell, who later became a great star for the Spartans when the Ironton team folded after the season. There were some great guys on that Spartans team.

Going to a Spartans game in the early 1930s was a great experience. They would yell and cheer when a good play occurred. It was quite thrilling for a young man—nothing like it is today. It's an altogether different ballgame. Back then they would hit them hard, and the whole team would play both offense and defense. Portsmouth fans were very loyal. I never heard anyone say anything bad about the Spartans, even when they lost. They were still a beloved bunch to everyone.

There wasn't all the razzmatazz then like there is today; it was just straight football. That's mainly what everybody was interested in. It was great to watch. Sometimes you'd find a few liquor bottles, but most of the fans were pretty well behaved. We had no bands, but somebody would always get up and lead the cheers. At that time, everybody in Portsmouth would get excited about the Spartans. They were treated like royalty. They were role models to us.

Some of the Spartans stayed in private homes while playing here. One or two of them were noted for going out and having a good time. I remember Father Lumpkin. He was quite a guy and a wonderful ballplayer. He loved to mingle. And on the field, he often played without a headgear. We also had a big tackle named George Christensen who was really tough. He'd break through any line there was. When we played the Chicago Bears here in Portsmouth [1932], they had Red Grange and Bronko Nagurski, the best bunch you ever saw, but our team played them to a 7-7 tie. To hold your own against Nagurski, who was considered the toughest guy in the league, and Red Grange, that was quite a feat.

Dutch Clark was probably the greatest Spartans player. Dutch was a quarterback at Colorado College before he came to Portsmouth. He was one of the first entries into the Pro Football Hall of Fame. He was just about as good as they come. Not only did we see our heroes play, we also saw other stars of the early pro game. We'd sometimes go down to the hotel where the visiting team was staying to see some of them.

Once, Ernie Nevers, the great back with the Chicago Cardinals, was at the hotel, so some of us young guys walked down to the hotel and sat down next to him. We talked to him for about an hour. He was just down-to-earth. You sort of think these great guys are on pedestals, but they're not. Most of them were really down-to-earth if you just went up to them and talked to them like an ordinary person.[2]

To see the stars of the NFL, a game ticket would cost a dollar and a half. That would get you the best seats—a dollar and a half. But if you could pass as a high school boy, it was fifty cents. After high school, I sometimes did that, I'm sorry to say. I guess I still owe them. Money was a big issue for the team, especially a small town like Portsmouth.

One of my last memories of the team was a game against the Cincinnati Reds. I traveled to Cincinnati to see them lose to a bad Reds team. They had no business losing to that team. Well, I came back with them on the train, and they all felt bad about losing. But they knew the team was in bad financial shape. They knew the team was probably going to have to leave Portsmouth in order to survive. Most of them didn't want to leave. They had a good opinion of us. They were just worshipped here.[3]

If they had won a championship, I think our big industries would've subsidized the team and had them stay. Most cities put a lot of emphasis on a football team or any professional team. We could've done what Green Bay did, where everybody has stock. We might've done that had the team won a championship, but the financial crisis came, and the players didn't get their money.

When the Spartans left, we all felt rather bad, but we just had to accept the fact that we couldn't support them anymore. It was explained to everyone that we just couldn't afford it. Somebody brought up the idea that the Selby Shoe Company, located here in town, who was paying over one thousand dollars for one page of advertisement in one of the leading magazines, should do something about saving the Spartans. They said, "Boy, if Selby would give that money to the Spartans, that might do it." One thousand dollars was a lot of money back then, but that was his main business, not football. Everybody was sad to see them go.

The team was sold to Detroit, where in 1935 they won the NFL championship. Most of those guys were old Spartans, and we were tickled to death that they won. Most of us had become Detroit fans because of the old Spartans. *Life* magazine had a famous photo of Dutch Clark in it once, and we were thrilled to see it. Everybody in Portsmouth wanted a copy of it.[4] The Spartans will always be remembered here. The Spartans were our shining glory, if we ever had such a thing.

The stadium in which the Spartans played is still there. I'm glad to see the high school team still uses it for all their games. We had a big discussion a while back where the city would donate the stadium to Shawnee State University. I thought they should because Shawnee State can get the money from the state whenever they need it. We always had a hard time keeping up that stadium. In fact, we let it deteriorate a few times, but it's fixed up pretty good right now. It's a pretty good stadium for a town this size.

We had a reunion for the old Spartans once [1970], and several players came back for that. I remember Father Lumpkin, Ox Emerson, and Glenn Presnell came back. It was wonderful to see them again. Sometimes I catch myself thinking about the old Spartans. Once in 1997, I was reading about the hullabaloo when the Green Bay Packers won the Super Bowl. I started thinking about the small-town rivalry between the Packers and the Spartans, so I wrote a poem. I guess I was inspired by the old Spartans. We have a poetry column in our paper every Sunday. So I submitted it, and they published it. It's called "Super Bowl Reflections" by Leo Blackburn. [Blackburn reads poem.]

> Here's to the Packers of Old Green Bay!
> Another Super Bowl they've won! Hooray!
> Numbers One and Two and Thirty-one,
> All three with Class-3 jobs well done!
>
> But here in Portsmouth, O-H-I-O
> Old Timers think long ago,
> When our Great Spartans took the field.
> And to the best teams would not yield.
>
> Our greatest joy in those old days
> Were those great Spartans' winning ways,
> They were the Heroes of the town,
> They brought this area great renown.
>
> Their greatest rival was Green Bay,
> And some of us to this late day,
> Remember well that fateful game
> When to River City the Packers came.
>
> December Four in Thirty-Two
> A date that signals derring-do,
> Then Portsmouth had a "bone to pick,"
> For old Green Bay we had to lick.
>
> That Game!—The likes will ne'r be seen!
> Our valiant Spartans smashed the Green

With just eleven warriors strong.
Revenge was sweet. Right won o'er Wrong!

Our Spartans struggled hard that day,
And 19 points finally came our way;
While old Green Bay a goose egg laid.
Yes!!! T'was the Greatest Game e'er Played!

Had Portsmouth kept the Spartans here
For us perhaps the world would cheer
As now it does for Old Green Bay.
Alas! Those years we can't replay!

And like the "rose of yesteryear,"
For Portsmouth, one must shed a tear;
Our Spartans to the Lions den!?!
Oh, those sad words, "It might have been."[5]

The Portsmouth Spartans were the high point athletically for our city. We'll never exceed that, and because it is a high point, I think they will always be remembered. Even when all the spectators are gone, they will still talk about the Spartans. There's still too much to talk about. As long as they write books and study the National Football League, then Portsmouth will always be mentioned. It was about as much a hero-worship town as you could find anywhere. I think the memory of the Spartans is going to be here forever.

Leo Blackburn was a state senator (1951–1952) and Portsmouth postmaster and helped found the Portsmouth Interstate Business College in 1946. Today the school is called the Southeastern Business College. A lifelong resident of Portsmouth, Leo passed away at the age of ninety on December 1, 2001.

Extra Point

Spartans Defense

The Portsmouth Spartans were always led by their aggressive defense during their short four-year career in the NFL. From 1930 to 1933, the Spartans had sixteen shutouts in fifty-one league games, giving up an average of only 7.76 points per game (396 points allowed). Their best year was in 1931, when they allowed a league-low 77 points and posted six shutouts in fourteen league games.

Earl "Dutch" Clark

Tailback-Quarterback, 1931–1932 Portsmouth Spartans, 1934–1938 Detroit Lions

> It was hard to get your money in Portsmouth, but I didn't blame them. It was during a depression and the people didn't have a lot of money, so I can't blame them.
>
> —Dutch Clark

Earl "Dutch" Clark (1906–1978) was born on October 11, 1906, in a small farming community in Fowler, Colorado. Always interested in sports, Clark went on to star in baseball, basketball, track, and football at tiny Colorado College. Despite playing for the small school, he was named a College All-American his senior year (1929). After working at his alma mater in 1930, he decided to give professional football a shot. He was signed by Potsy Clark to play for the Portsmouth (Ohio) Spartans of the National Football League in 1931. After two successful seasons and too many missed paychecks, he left to become football coach and athletic director at the Colorado School of Mines. He missed the historic and hastily arranged indoor play-off game in 1932 against the Chicago Bears and the entire 1933 season.

After the 1933 NFL season, the Spartans were sold to G. A. Richards, who moved the franchise to Detroit and renamed the team the Lions. Richards then convinced Clark to come out of retirement and play for the Lions. Clark went on to play five more years, leading the Lions to the 1935 NFL Championship and becoming a player-coach during the 1937 and 1938 seasons (his record was 14-8). He then went on to coach the Cleveland Rams for four seasons (1939–1942), compiling a record of 16-26-2. Clark was a charter member of the Pro Football Hall of Fame in 1963. Dutch Clark was interviewed for one hour by a Detroit television station in 1962. This interview was found in the archives of the Pro Football Hall of Fame.

I WAS BORN IN A SMALL FARMING TOWN IN FOWLER, COLORADO. MY father was a farmer. My parents ended up having five children: two girls and three boys. I was the fourth of the five kids. I didn't get to play much sports growing up because my father died when I was fourteen years old, and at that time I started working on the railroad. I wanted to help the family, and I wasn't thinking about going to school, but I changed my mind later and went on to high school. That's where I started to play sports, including football.

In high school, I tried every sport I could. I played football, basketball, baseball, track, and one year I even lettered in tennis. Once I got started playing, I figured it was something I really liked, so I figured I would go on to college and maybe go into coaching. I thought football was my best sport. Some thought it was basketball. One year we won the state title and were invited to the National Interscholastic Basketball Tournament in Chicago. I remember we beat a team from Newton, Kansas, that was considerably better than us. We saw them the night before scoring a lot of points, so we decided to hold on to the ball [no shot clock]. We held the ball, and they stayed back in their zone defense. They never challenged us. I think the half ended 6-1. We finally beat them 13-11. We did end up losing in the finals, but it was a great experience.

Our football team never won a state title, but we came close a couple of times. During my senior year, I started to get some attention from several colleges. For a while, I thought I was headed to Michigan until a guy from Northwestern talked to me. He convinced me Northwestern was the place for me. So a week before I was to leave for Michigan, I was on a plane going to Northwestern. But I didn't last very long at Northwestern. I took the entrance exams and then I left, so I was there for about two weeks. I was getting homesick, and I missed the mountains very much. I left Northwestern and enrolled at Colorado College. It was a small liberal arts school with about 500 students.

While at Colorado College, I played baseball, basketball, track, and football. Our football team used the single wing, and I played left halfback. I called the signals and ran with the ball from that position. We also threw quite a bit. We weren't a very big team, and we didn't have much depth, so we had to throw it to some extent. I liked it that way. It made me a better all-around player. I think that helped me later when I played pro ball.

One of our most famous college games was against Denver College, and I ended up scoring all the points. Early in the game, I fumbled a punt into our own end zone and fell on it for a safety. They led 2-0. Then late in the game, with about thirty seconds remaining, I kicked a field goal to beat them 3-2. I scored all the points, but I'm not proud of the two points I gave them.

I think one thing most people don't know is that I was blind in one eye. I never noticed it until I got to college. I know I would be considered blind in that eye today if I played, but it never hindered me in football. I made All–Rocky Mountain halfback three times, and my senior year I made a few All-American teams. One selection really surprised me. A writer from the AP by the name of Alan Gould put me on his first-team All-American team. Because he was an eastern writer and most of the All-American teams were loaded with eastern stars, he was criticized for selecting me. Frankly, I thought he was crazy, too, but it was nice to be honored.[1]

After graduating from Colorado College in 1930, I ended up coaching there. I was making a few dollars, so I enjoyed it. Then in 1931, I was contacted by Potsy Clark, who offered me a chance to play pro football for the Portsmouth Spartans. I was always curious to see if I could play with the best players. I played at a small school, and that, I think, was one of the reasons I made up my mind to play pro football. I also wanted to prove that the eastern writer who voted me All-American wasn't that crazy. That was my motivation.

I ended up signing with the Portsmouth Spartans [1931] for $140 a game. I didn't always get it, but that's what I signed for. It was hard to get your money in Portsmouth, but I didn't blame them. It was during a Depression, and the people didn't have a lot of money, so I can't blame them. The team tried to save money, too. We traveled by bus instead of train. We'd get on the bus early in the morning, then we'd stop two or three times along the way to practice our plays. Potsy would tell us to bring our shoes on the bus because once he saw a smooth open field, we'd stop and run some signals. Then we'd get back on the bus and continue down the road. Of course, you're perspiring, but nobody seemed to mind.

Potsy was always thinking like that. He was ahead of his time. When I first came to Portsmouth, we had a lot of old pros on the club, so Potsy had us out there experimenting. That was something that they never heard of—professional football teams scrimmaging (our first-team players against the second-team players).

The game at that time is pretty much the same now. It's about blocking and tackling. The only huge difference is we played both ways. You would start the game on offense and defense. Our equipment was a little heavier, too. Your trousers were a heavy canvas, and your headgear was a heavy leather. Now you have the hard plastic helmet to wear. You always wore the high-top shoes. I think the shoes were much heavier than today. Now you can wear sneakers.

We were starting to build a good team in Portsmouth, and I made All-Pro my two years there. At the end of the 1932 season, we tied for first place with the Chicago Bears. They decided to play a championship game between the two teams after the last regular season game. Because this game wasn't on the schedule, I had to miss it. I wanted to go into coaching, so when the Colorado School of Mines asked me to become athletic director and head football and basketball coach, I decided to take it. I thought the season would be over, not thinking they would schedule another game. So my college wouldn't let me play in the game. The Spartans lost a close one 9-0.

Because of my job at the college, I decided to not play football for the Spartans in 1933. I wasn't very happy about not getting paid in Portsmouth, and the money situation wasn't getting any better there. It wasn't worth worrying about, so I didn't go back. That's one of the reasons I quit.

The following year, the Spartans were sold to G. A. Richards, a radio man from Detroit. He moved the team there and renamed them the Lions. His first move was to get me to play football again. He made me a great offer, so I came back. He was a great friend to me and the rest of the football club. I think he'd do almost anything to see that we win. He treated the boys real nice. It was so much different than Portsmouth. It was very wonderful to be up there and play for Richards and the city of Detroit.

The Lions were a first-class operation from the moment I signed with them. The whole setup was so much better than Portsmouth. At first we didn't draw too well. Professional football was just getting started in the city. They had a few earlier teams, but it was still fairly new. We started the season [1934] with seven straight shutouts and ten straight wins, but we ended up losing our last three games by 3 points each and missed out on winning the championship. But our success that first year did a great job of starting pro football and continuing it here in the city of Detroit.

The following year, we finally put it all together, and we won the NFL title. We beat the New York Giants 26-7 in the championship game. The city ended up having a couple of champions that year. The hockey team and the Detroit Tigers also won titles.[2] After the season, I felt a little banged up and was considering retiring, but I used to consider quitting after almost every game. As the years wore on, it took me a whole week to get over those bumps and bruises. So each week I would say, "This is my last year." But come summer, you're feeling pretty good, and playing football again sounds like a good idea.

I was always treated well by the Detroit fans and press. Once during practice, we had a photographer named Bill Kuenzel from the *Detroit News* come out. He was taking photos for a story. Well, he took a photo of me from the side, a profile shot. I was just kneeling on the sidelines watching our defense run a few drills. Bill just snapped it. It turned out wonderful. It was in the photo section, and the newspaper got a ton of requests for the photo. It then appeared in *Life* magazine. I don't know whether he thought I was photogenic or what. He came out again and must've snapped a hundred more, but he never had a good one like the first one. It was just something that happened.

At the end of my career with the Lions, I became a player-coach. Potsy was still the head coach, but I helped coach the backs, and George Christensen helped with the line. I learned a lot from Potsy. He was quite a little character, a feisty little guy. I thought he did a great job coaching. He was great at getting a ball club ready for a game. I don't think we ever went out on the field when we weren't ready to play. He'd give us pep talks all week long, not just on game days. I always thought coaching was tough. When I left the Lions to become the head coach of the Cleveland Rams in 1939, I found that out. Our offense was much simpler, and we didn't work at it year-round the way coaches do now.

After coaching the Rams for four years, I went out west and coached the Seattle Bombers for one year. Then I bounced around for a couple of years before returning to Detroit. I became head football coach and athletic director of the University of Detroit.

My best ballplayer there had to be Teddy Marchibroda, who was a terrific quarterback.[3] But we had trouble recruiting because if Michigan, Michigan State, or Notre Dame wanted a boy, well, you didn't get him. So it was difficult to compete with those schools.

I still follow the game closely. I attend as many Lions and University of Detroit games as I possibly can. Lately, I've been going to some local high school games. A couple of my boys played high school football. I used to talk to them a little, but now I stay out of the way. The coach tells them what they are supposed to do. It would be silly for me to try and tell the boy something, and he goes over and says, "Well, Pop said this." The coach would probably run him off the field. The coach does an excellent job with the boys—better than I would do—so I just keep my mouth shut.

I think kids today have a great advantage in playing football than when I played. They can start out when they are young and play Little

League football. The coaches do a great job in getting the kids in shape and teaching them the fundamentals. I think that's better than going out and playing sandlot football. The kids then can go into junior high and high school much better prepared. I think if a boy wanted to play, there'd be nothing better for him than to start on one of those Little League teams.

Dutch Clark made All-NFL in six of his seven seasons and led the league in scoring for three seasons: 1932, 1935, and 1936. Clark called signals, played tailback, and became the NFL's last dropkicking specialist. He was selected as a charter member of the Pro Football Hall of Fame in 1963. Clark died on August 5, 1978, at the age of seventy-one.

Extra Point

What Others Are Saying about Dutch Clark

Potsy Clark on Dutch Clark: "He is a rabbit in the brush heap when he gets in the secondary. Just when you expect him to be smothered, he's free of tacklers."[4]

Bronko Nagurski on Dutch Clark: "He looks like the easiest man on the field to tackle. The first time I tried to tackle him I thought I'd break him in two. But when I closed my arms all I was holding was air."[5]

Lester H. Higgins was hired by his brother-in-law Ralph Hay to be team treasurer of the Canton Bulldogs. He served in that capacity from 1919 to 1923. The Bulldogs went on to win back-to-back NFL championships in 1922 and 1923. Photo courtesy of Dr. James King

Joseph F. Carr was an assistant sports editor of the Ohio State Journal *and manager of the Columbus Panhandles professional football team, before becoming president of the NFL in 1921. He stayed in office until his death in 1939. Carr was inducted into the Pro Football Hall of Fame in 1963.* Photo courtesy of the Pro Football Hall of Fame

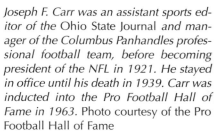

Fritz Pollard was the first African American backfield player elected to Walter Camp's All-American team in 1916, while at Brown University. He went on to become the first African American head coach in NFL history in 1921, when he was co–head coach with Elgie Tobin of the 1921 Akron Pros. Pollard was elect-ed to the College Football Hall of Fame in 1954. Photo courtesy of the College Football Hall of Fame

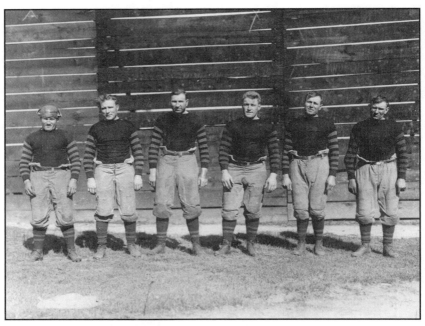

The six Nesser brothers played for the Columbus Panhandles. This photo is from 1916, before the Panhandles joined the NFL. From left to right: Ted, halfback and tackle; Al, end and guard; Fred, end and halfback; Frank, fullback; Phil, tackle; and John, quarterback. None of the Nesser brothers ever played college football; instead they all worked in the Panhandle Division of the Pennsylvania Railroad. Photo courtesy of the Ohio Historical Society

George "Hobby" Kinderdine played center for the Dayton Triangles in the NFL from 1920 to 1929. Kinderdine never played football in high school or college. Photo courtesy of the Pro Football Hall of Fame

Lee Fenner played end for the Dayton Triangles in the NFL from 1920 to 1927 and 1929. Fenner never played college football. In this photo, Fenner is wearing his Dayton Triangles jersey, circa the mid-1920s. Photo courtesy of Mark Fenner

Ike Roy Martin played halfback at William Jewel College in Missouri before playing pro football for the Fort Wayne (Indiana) Friars and the Canton Bulldogs. Martin played just one year in the NFL, with the 1920 Canton Bulldogs. Photo courtesy of the Pro Football Hall of Fame

Arda Bowser played fullback in the NFL for the Canton Bulldogs in 1922 and the Cleveland Indians in 1923. In 1922 Bowser helped lead the Bulldogs to a record of 10-0-2 and the NFL championship. In this photo, Bowser is wearing his 1922 Canton Bulldogs jersey. Photo courtesy of the Pro Football Hall of Fame

Art Haley played running back in the NFL for the Canton Bulldogs in 1920, the Dayton Triangles in 1921, and the Akron Pros in 1923. Haley was a star at the University of Akron and was inducted into the school's Sports Hall of Fame in 1979. Photo courtesy of the Canton Repository

Walter Lingo, owner of the Oorang Dog Kennels, located in LaRue, Ohio, purchased an NFL franchise in 1922 for one hundred dollars. The Oorang Indians played just two seasons in the NFL, 1922–1923. Photo courtesy of Bob Lingo

William Guthery, Sr., played end as a senior for the LaRue High School Football Team. Guthery is in the front row sitting down, first one on the left. Photo courtesy of William Guthery, Sr.

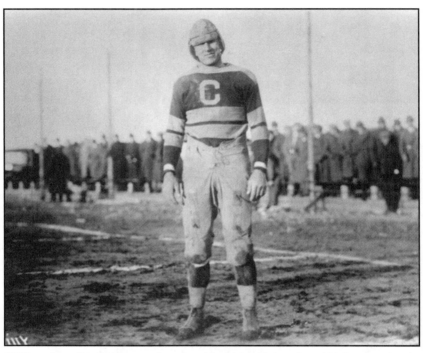

William Roy "Link" Lyman played tackle at the University of Nebraska, despite not having played in high school. He went on to play eleven seasons in the NFL with the Canton Bulldogs (1922–1923, 1925); the Cleveland Bulldogs (1924); the Frankford Yellowjackets (1925); and the Chicago Bears (1926–1928, 1930–1931, 1933–1934). Lyman won four NFL titles and was elected to the Pro Football Hall of Fame in 1964. This photo shows him in his Canton Bulldogs uniform. Photo courtesy of the Pro Football Hall of Fame

Hal Broda played end at Brown University before playing three games with the 1927 Cleveland Bulldogs. Those three contests make up his entire NFL career. Photo courtesy of the Pro Football Hall of Fame

Glenn Presnell was an All-American halfback at the University of Nebraska be-fore playing nine seasons of professional football with the Ironton (Ohio) Tanks (1928–1930), the Portsmouth Spartans (1931–1933) and the Detroit Lions (1934–1936). Photo Courtesy of Mary Presnell

Earl "Dutch" Clark was an All-American halfback at Colorado College before playing seven seasons in the NFL with the Portsmouth Spartans (1931–1932) and the Detroit Lions (1934–1938). Clark was elected to the Pro Football Hall of Fame in 1963. This photo was taken before the Lions season opener in 1937. Photo courtesy of the author's collection

This photo is of the Portsmouth Spartans reunion held on August 4, 1970. The city of Portsmouth honored the team by renaming the stadium Spartans Stadium. Former Spartans who returned were: (top row, left to right) Roy "Father" Lumpkin, Harry Ebding, Glenn Presnell, Ox Emerson, and Popeye Wager; (bottom row, left to right) Jim Steen, Cyrus Kahl, Ace Gutowsky, John Schneller, and Jack Johnson. Photo courtesy of the author's collection

Norris Steverson became the first-ever player from Arizona State University to play in the NFL, as a halfback with the 1934 Cincinnati Reds. It was the only year he played in the NFL. Photo courtesy of Margaret Steverson

Cyrus Kahl

Blocking Back,
1930–1931 Portsmouth Spartans

Cyrus never intended to be a ballplayer. He came to Portsmouth to earn
a few dollars while waiting to learn if he passed the bar exam. He was
going to be a lawyer.

—Alma Kahl

*Cyrus Kahl (1904–1971) was born on November 29, 1904, in Heaton,
North Dakota, but moved to Alexandria, Minnesota, as a young boy. After high school, he enrolled at the University of Minnesota but left because
sports interfered with his studies. He transferred to North Dakota University, where he played football, studied law, and graduated with honors.
While awaiting the results of his bar exam, Kahl jumped at an offer to earn
one hundred dollars a game playing for the National Football League's
Portsmouth Spartans.*

*Kahl's career was brief—the 1930 season and one game in 1931—
but his stay in Portsmouth was not. In 1930, a local lawyer and Spartans
fan offered Kahl a position in his law firm. He accepted and settled down
to a law career in Portsmouth. It was there that Cyrus met his wife,
Alma, and they lived in Portsmouth until his death in 1971. Alma Kahl
was interviewed by the author for twenty minutes at her home in
Portsmouth on June 30, 2000.*

CYRUS KAHL EARNED HIS LIVING FROM THE TIME HE WAS A YOUNG BOY
through athletics. He grew up in Alexandria, Minnesota. He was
always playing sports. He was very good in high school and decided to stay close to home for college. He went to the University of

Minnesota, but he didn't stay there very long because he wanted to be a lawyer. The school had him doing too much, and he didn't have enough time to study. He went to school from eight till twelve, and then he would eat his lunch. He would then practice from one until five. After dinner, the athletic department had him working from six-thirty to eleven. He thought this was a little too much, so he transferred to North Dakota University. I don't think football was that important to him.

While at North Dakota, his schedule was much better. He had enough time to study. He was able to play football and study law much better at North Dakota. He ended up graduating with honors. At this time, he was getting ready to take the bar exam. He wasn't even thinking about playing professional football. He was only an average player. So in the summer of 1930, he took the bar exams in both Minnesota and North Dakota.

While waiting for his scores to come in, he got an offer to play pro football with the Portsmouth Spartans in southern Ohio. I was in high school at this time. Because it would take some time for his scores to come in, he thought he could make a few dollars playing football. A few dollars is what he made. Cyrus made one hundred dollars a game. Back in that time, you did well to get a hundred dollars. He was glad to get it because he had no money. I know he never intended to be a ballplayer. He only came to Portsmouth to earn some extra money. Once he got his results from the bar, he was going to leave.

He enjoyed his time with the Spartans. That team united the city more than anything else. Everybody went to the games on Sundays. Everyone in town or in the county was interested in the Spartans. We were very proud of the team. Cyrus always said that everyone was very nice to the ballplayers. Also, every Sunday after a home game, several families would invite the boys over for dinner. The players were very popular.

Like I said before, Cyrus never intended to be a ballplayer, but playing for Portsmouth did change his life. During that 1930 season in Portsmouth, he met a gentleman named Mr. Skelton. He was a partner in a law firm here in town. He was also a big Spartans fan, so he invited Cyrus to join his law firm. Well, Cyrus thought this was a great idea. He now had a job and stayed in Portsmouth for the rest of his life. Sometimes I wonder what would've happened if Cyrus didn't come to Portsmouth to play pro football. Or what if he received his test scores sooner, before Mr. Skelton made him the job offer?

I ended up meeting Cyrus a couple of years after I graduated from West Virginia University. We met at a party through some mutual friends. We lived in Portsmouth until he passed away in 1971. I've continued to live here ever since.

I remember we had a reunion for the Spartans in 1970. I can remember hearing "The Spartans are coming" all summer. It didn't sink in until about the weekend before they were to arrive. Suddenly, you realized all those people were coming. So we had one of the dinners here at our home. I was delighted to meet each one of them. They were all very nice. They were all highly intelligent men. They had such a great time. The town honored the team that weekend by renaming the stadium where they played Spartans Stadium.

Today, the town talks about the Spartans very freely, as if it was just a few years ago. The town is very proud of them. They remember the team with fondness, and they always smile when they talk about the team. We'll always remember them. I know I'll always remember them with fondness.

Cyrus Kahl played in twelve NFL games with the Portsmouth Spartans over a two-year span (1930–1931). He continued to live in Portsmouth until his death in July of 1971, less than a year after the Spartans' 1970 team reunion. In 1980 Kahl was inducted into the North Dakota State College of Science Athletic Hall of Fame. After planning to stay for only a few football games, Cyrus stayed in Portsmouth for forty-one years. His widow, Alma Kahl, still lives in Portsmouth.

Extra Point

A Good-Bye Poem to Father Lumpkin

Oh Lumpkin, Father Lumpkin to Whom the Spartans pray,
We had you for a moment, Oh, why could you not stay?
You lifted up our spirit, Made Peerless grid fans gay,
But now that you have left us, We'll paint the Floodwall grey.
—From the fans of the Portsmouth Spartans[1]

Norris Steverson

Halfback, 1934 Cincinnati Reds

I was very much looking forward to playing with Red Grange
and Bronko Nagurski; they were the best.

—Norris Steverson

*Norris Steverson (1910–2004) was interviewed by the author for forty
minutes on July 5, 2002, at his home in Mesa, Arizona. Steverson was
born on July 20, 1910, and raised by his grandparents in Mesa. Steverson attended Arizona State Teachers College, now Arizona State University, where he earned an honorable mention as All-American in 1931. He
taught physical education at the college after graduating and figured his
football career was over.*

*Then, early in 1934, Steverson joined a team of Arizona all-stars in
Phoenix to face the barnstorming Chicago Bears, the reigning NFL
champions. The Bears crushed the pickup all-star team, but Steverson's
play impressed Bears coach George Halas enough that he signed Steverson to a contract after the game. Alas, the signing marked the high point
of Steverson's National Football League career: Halas sold his contract
to the woeful Cincinnati Reds before the start of the 1934 season.*

*Bronko Nagurski, Red Grange, and the Bears finished that regular
season undefeated; Steverson and the Reds never finished. Plagued by
poor play on the field and poor attendance at the gate, the Reds folded
after a 0-8 start. Steverson played out the year with the semipro Tulsa
Oilers, then returned to Arizona to resume his career as a teacher and
coach. By playing for the Reds, Steverson became the first player from
Arizona State University to play in the NFL.*

After his retirement from pro football, Steverson began teaching at Arizona State. In 1950 he founded the ASU men's gymnastics club team and guided it through the first decade of varsity competition until 1968. He has been associated with Arizona State as a player, coach, teacher, alumni, and fan for over seventy-five years. In 1975 Steverson was inducted as a charter member of the ASU Sports Hall of Fame.

I GREW UP ON THE WEST COAST AT A TIME WHEN FOOTBALL WAS JUST getting started. We didn't have any real pro teams in Arizona, but the colleges played. My mother was a teacher, and my father held several jobs. He worked as a farmer, bartender, and was an engineer for awhile. Then, when I was about ten years old, they divorced. I was an only child, so they sent me to Mesa, Arizona, to live with my grandparents.

I was pretty good at all the major sports. We didn't play much golf or tennis, just the major sports. We played baseball, basketball, track, and of course, football. Football was always my favorite sport, and that continued well into high school. I ended up lettering in all four sports in high school, and I thought I could continue in college. So after graduation, I decided to go to Arizona State Teachers College, which is now Arizona State University.

Arizona State let me play all four sports, which was fine with me. I loved keeping busy, and that's what I did. But it was an off-the-field event that made me very popular around campus. In Hollywood at that time, the movies named Clara Bow as the "It Girl." So Arizona State held a contest to find the school's "It Girl" and "It Man." So as a freshman, I won the "It Man." I beat out the whole campus for this prestigious title. Everybody got to know me really well after that.

I was considered a triple-threat player while at Arizona State. I could run, pass, and kick. In 1930 I was elected captain. That was a nice honor for me. We struggled as a team my first couple of years, but we put it all together in 1931. Our crowning moment came against our chief rival, Arizona, that year. The school hadn't beaten Arizona since 1899, and we needed that win to finish in first place in the newly established Border Conference.

I remember the week leading up to the game. The student body was very concerned if we could win, so we wanted to win very badly. We had the ball first, but we couldn't do anything with it, so we punted. As Arizona's offense got rolling after our punt, my heart started to sink. But we held them, and on the following punt, I returned it for about 35 yards to set up a touchdown. From then on, I felt good about our chances.

I had a hand in all three touchdowns we scored that day, and we beat them 19-6. I think it was the school's biggest win, and I think it was another several years until we beat Arizona again [1949]. The school newspaper in Tucson said there were three reasons the Wildcats lost the game: Steverson, Steverson, and Steverson. At the end of that season, I was named to the first All–Border Conference team and won honorable mention honors for All-American. This made me even more popular on campus. I remember years later when I had to make some phone calls for a class reunion, I couldn't believe how many people remembered me from my football accomplishments.

Before my junior year, our athletic director, Aaron McCreary, wanted to talk to me about my future. He told me if I make physical education my major, then the school would hire me after I graduated. So I gave it a try. It took a lot of hard work, but I got it done. After graduation, I taught physical education at Arizona State.

Since we didn't have any good pro teams in Arizona, I never really thought about playing pro football. But in early 1934, George Halas and his Chicago Bears were barnstorming the country, and they were going to stop in Phoenix and play a game against a team of Arizona all-stars. I was contacted by Cecil Mulleneaux, who played at ASC in Flagstaff [Arizona State College at Flagstaff, now Northern Arizona University] and who was playing with the Cincinnati Reds of the NFL. He was in charge of putting the Arizona team together, and he asked me to play.[1] Well, I hadn't played any competitive football in over two years since I graduated, so I thought I'd give it a try.

Despite getting beat pretty bad [55-0], I was voted the top all-star from the Arizona team, and the vote was done by the Bears players. George Halas was so impressed by me that he signed me to a contract with the Bears after the game. I was going to get ninety dollars a game for the 1934 season, which today doesn't sound like a lot of money. It was a tremendous thrill to sign with the Bears. I was very much looking forward to playing with Red Grange and Bronko Nagurski; they were the best. Just being part of the Bears was more than I could have imagined. I couldn't wait.

But it never happened. Right before training camp with the Bears, my contract was sold to the Cincinnati Reds. Cecil Mulleneaux needed players, so he had Halas trade me to the Reds. I was very disappointed about being traded. Sometime in the mid-seventies, Halas visited Arizona State and told me he always regretted trading me. That made me feel a little better about the whole thing.

I did play for the Cincinnati Reds in 1934, but that didn't last too long. The Reds weren't a very good team. We were absolutely terrible. We didn't win a game, and halfway through the season, they had money trouble and disbanded. The league moved the team to St. Louis to finish out the rest of the season.[2] I decided not to play for the St. Louis team. After the Reds disbanded, I was on my way home to Arizona when I was contacted by a friend to see if I wanted to play a few games with the semipro Tulsa [Oklahoma] Oilers. It was on my way home, so I agreed. They paid me a little bit, but nothing special.

I was very proud that I played professional football in the NFL, but I think it wasn't the lifestyle for me. There was too much downtime. I wanted to keep busy. I was always good at observing and analyzing sport activities. I guess that's what made me want to teach and coach. I spent over forty years teaching and coaching at USC, Arizona, and Arizona State. I coached swimming, tennis, gymnastics, and football at Arizona State. Later, before I retired, I even taught a class on trail riding because it was one thing I always wanted to do.

I've pretty much lived near Mesa all my life. I've always loved living out here in Arizona. I met my second wife, Margaret, here. She too was a graduate of Arizona State, and in 1945 we got married. In December of 2003, we celebrated our fifty-eighth wedding anniversary. My memory hasn't been that good lately, but Margaret's is very sharp, so I'm glad she is here to help me.

I still enjoy the game of football. The style of the game hasn't changed; you've still got to get the ball into the end zone. I try to watch a few games a week when they are on. I used to go to all the Arizona State games here. I had a streak going for about twenty-five years, never missing a home game, until about the last couple of years when my health kept me away. They were nicknamed the Bulldogs when I played, so I try to keep up with them now.

Norris Steverson played just five games with the 1934 Cincinnati Reds until they disbanded because of financial problems. On July 20, 2003, Norris celebrated his ninety-third birthday with his wife of fifty-eight years, Margaret Steverson. On March 23, 2004, Steverson passed away in Mesa, Arizona, at the age of ninety-three.

Extra Point

The Worst Team in NFL History!

The 1934 Cincinnati Reds were arguably the worst team in NFL history. Not only did they finish with a record of 0-8, they were outscored by their opponents 243-10! They scored only one touchdown and one field goal in eight games. The 1976 Tampa Bay Buccaneers, who went 0-14 in their first season, still scored 75 points in their first eight games.

Overtime

FTER THE CINCINNATI REDS FOLDED IN 1934, THE STATE OF OHIO didn't see another franchise in the NFL until 1937, when the Cleveland Rams joined the league. It wouldn't be until World War II that the state of Ohio had a team win an NFL title, when the 1945 Rams defeated the Washington Redskins 15-14.

During the first fifteen seasons of the NFL, the state of Ohio played a major role in the development of professional football. Even though the nickname "Cradle of Pro Football" was gone by 1935, for the 645 different men and the 9 different cities—Akron, Canton, Cincinnati, Cleveland, Columbus, Dayton, LaRue, Portsmouth, and Toledo—who played in the NFL during that Old Leather period, these were precious years and memories worth remembering.

Appendix

Complete Standings, Team Rosters, Game Results, and Attendance Figures for all Ohio Teams in the National Football League, 1920–1935

Sample Key

Year: Team name: (Overall record, place in league standings)

Head coach—Coach's name
Home field—Where they played home games

Roster   Results

Player—Position   Date of game-Opponent-Score-Crowd

Each player's name—Position played

Position abbreviation
TB—Tailback
HB—Halfback
FB—Fullback
WB—Wingback
BB—Blockingback
T—Tackle
G—Guard
C—Center
E—End

* 1920—No official standings were maintained for the 1920 season, and the championship was awarded to the Akron Pros in a League meeting on April 30, 1921. Clubs played schedules that included games against nonleague teams.

(Appendix information courtesy of Total Football II,[1] The Pro Football Encyclopedia,[2] *and the* 2004 NFL Record & Fact Book[3])

NFL Standings 1920–1935 (Ohio Teams in Bold)

1920 APFA*	W-L-T	Pct.
Akron Pros	8-0-3	1.000
Decatur Staleys	10-1-2	.909
Buffalo All-Americans	9-1-1	.900
Chicago Cardinals	6-2-2	.750
Rock Island Independents	6-2-2	.750
Dayton Triangles	5-2-2	.714
Rochester Jeffersons	6-3-2	.667
Canton Bulldogs	7-4-2	.636
Detroit Heralds	2-3-3	.400
Cleveland Tigers	2-4-2	.333
Chicago Tigers	2-5-1	.286
Hammond Pros	2-5-0	.286
Columbus Panhandles	2-6-2	.250
Muncie Flyers	0-1-0	.000

1921 APFA	W-L-T	Pct.
Chicago Staleys	9-1-1	.900
Buffalo All-Americans	9-1-2	.900
Akron Pros	8-3-1	.727
Canton Bulldogs	5-2-3	.714
Rock Island Independents	4-2-1	.667
Evansville Crimson Giants	3-2-0	.600
Green Bay Packers	3-2-1	.600
Dayton Triangles	4-4-1	.500
Chicago Cardinals	3-3-2	.500
Rochester Jeffersons	2-3-0	.400
Cleveland Indians	3-5-0	.375
Washington Senators	1-2-0	.333
Cincinnati Celts	1-3-0	.250
Hammond Pros	1-3-1	.250
Minneapolis Marines	1-3-0	.250
Detroit Heralds	1-5-1	.167
Columbus Panhandles	1-8-0	.111
Tonawanda Kardex	0-1-0	.000
Muncie Flyers	0-2-0	.000
Louisville Brecks	0-2-0	.000
New York Giants	0-2-0	.000

1922 NFL	W-L-T	Pct.
Canton Bulldogs	10-0-2	1.000
Chicago Bears	9-3-0	.750
Chicago Cardinals	8-3-0	.727
Toledo Maroons	5-2-2	.714
Rock Island Independents	4-2-1	.667
Racine Legion	6-4-1	.600
Dayton Triangles	4-3-1	.571
Green Bay Packers	4-3-3	.571
Buffalo All-Americans	5-4-1	.556
Akron Pros	3-5-2	.375
Milwaukee Badgers	2-4-3	.333
Oorang Indians	3-6-0	.333
Minneapolis Marines	1-3-0	.250
Louisville Brecks	1-3-0	.250
Evansville Crimson Giants	0-3-0	.000
Rochester Jeffersons	0-4-1	.000
Hammond Pros	0-5-1	.000
Columbus Panhandles	0-8-0	.000

1923 NFL	W-L-T	Pct.
Canton Bulldogs	11-0-1	1.000
Chicago Bears	9-2-1	.818
Green Bay Packers	7-2-1	.778
Milwaukee Badgers	7-2-3	.778
Cleveland Indians	3-1-3	.750
Chicago Cardinals	8-4-0	.667
Duluth Kelleys	4-3-0	.571
Buffalo All-Americans	5-4-3	.556
Columbus Tigers	5-4-1	.556
Racine Legion	4-4-2	.500
Toledo Maroons	3-3-2	.500
Rock Island Independents	2-3-3	.400
Minneapolis Marines	2-5-2	.286
St. Louis All-Stars	1-4-2	.200
Hammond Pros	1-5-1	.167
Dayton Triangles	1-6-1	.143
Akron Indians	1-6-0	.143
Oorang Indians	1-10-0	.091
Louisville Brecks	0-3-0	.000
Rochester Jeffersons	0-4-0	.000

1924 NFL	W-L-T	Pct.
Cleveland Bulldogs	7-1-1	.875
Chicago Bears	6-1-4	.857
Frankford Yellowjackets	11-2-1	.846
Duluth Kelleys	5-1-0	.833
Rock Island Independents	5-2-2	.714
Green Bay Packers	7-4-0	.636
Racine Legion	4-3-3	.571

Chicago Cardinals	5-4-1	.556
Buffalo Bisons	6-5-0	.545
Columbus Tigers	4-4-0	.500
Hammond Pros	2-2-1	.500
Milwaukee Badgers	5-8-0	.385
Akron Indians	2-6-0	.250
Dayton Triangles	2-6-0	.250
Kansas City Blues	2-7-0	.222
Kenosha Maroons	0-4-1	.000
Minneapolis Marines	0-6-0	.000
Rochester Jeffersons	0-7-0	.000

1925 NFL	W-L-T	Pct.
Chicago Cardinals	11-2-1	.846
Pottsville Maroons	10-2-0	.833
Detroit Panthers	8-2-2	.800
New York Giants	8-4-0	.667
Akron Indians	4-2-2	.667
Frankford Yellowjackets	13-7-0	.650
Chicago Bears	9-5-3	.643
Rock Island Independents	5-3-3	.625
Green Bay Packers	8-5-0	.615
Providence Steamrollers	6-5-1	.545
Canton Bulldogs	4-4-0	.500
Cleveland Bulldogs	5-8-1	.385
Kansas City Cowboys	2-5-1	.286
Hammond Pros	1-4-0	.200
Buffalo Bisons	1-6-2	.143
Duluth Kelleys	0-3-0	.000
Rochester Jeffersons	0-6-1	.000
Milwaukee Badgers	0-6-0	.000
Dayton Triangles	0-7-1	.000
Columbus Tigers	0-9-0	.000

1926 NFL	W-L-T	Pct.
Frankford Yellowjackets	14-1-2	.933
Chicago Bears	12-1-3	.923
Pottsville Maroons	10-2-2	.833
Kansas City Cowboys	8-3-0	.727
Green Bay Packers	7-3-3	.700
Los Angeles Buccaneers	6-3-1	.667
New York Giants	8-4-1	.667
Duluth Eskimos	6-5-3	.545
Buffalo Rangers	4-4-2	.500
Chicago Cardinals	5-6-1	.455
Providence Steamrollers	5-7-1	.417
Detroit Panthers	4-6-2	.400
Hartford Blues	3-7-0	.300
Brooklyn Lions	3-8-0	.273

Milwaukee Badgers	2-7-0	.222
Akron Pros	1-4-3	.200
Dayton Triangles	1-4-1	.200
Racine Tornadoes	1-4-0	.200
Columbus Tigers	**1-6-0**	**.143**
Canton Bulldogs	**1-9-3**	**.100**
Hammond Pros	0-4-0	.000
Louisville Colonels	0-4-0	.000

1927 NFL	W-L-T	Pct.
New York Giants	11-1-1	.917
Green Bay Packers	7-2-1	.778
Chicago Bears	9-3-2	.750
Cleveland Bulldogs	**8-4-1**	**.667**
Providence Steamrollers	8-5-1	.615
New York Yankees	7-8-1	.467
Frankford Yellowjackets	6-9-3	.400
Pottsville Maroons	5-8-0	.385
Chicago Cardinals	3-7-1	.300
Dayton Triangles	**1-6-1**	**.143**
Duluth Eskimos	1-8-0	.111
Buffalo Bisons	0-5-0	.000

1928 NFL	W-L-T	Pct.
Providence Steamrollers	8-1-2	.889
Frankford Yellowjackets	11-3-2	.786
Detroit Wolverines	7-2-1	.778
Green Bay Packers	6-4-3	.600
Chicago Bears	7-5-1	.583
New York Giants	4-7-2	.364
New York Yankees	4-8-1	.333
Pottsville Maroons	2-8-0	.200
Chicago Cardinals	1-5-0	.167
Dayton Triangles	**0-7-0**	**.000**

1929 NFL	W-L-T	Pct.
Green Bay Packers	12-0-1	1.000
New York Giants	13-1-1	.929
Frankford Yellowjackets	10-4-5	.714
Chicago Cardinals	6-6-1	.500
Boston Bulldogs	4-4-0	.500
Staten Island Stapletons	3-4-3	.429
Providence Steamrollers	4-6-2	.400
Orange Tornadoes	3-5-4	.375
Chicago Bears	4-9-2	.308
Buffalo Bisons	1-7-1	.125
Minneapolis Redjackets	1-9-0	.100
Dayton Triangles	**0-6-0**	**.000**

1930 NFL	W-L-T	Pct.
Green Bay Packers	10-3-1	.796
New York Giants	13-4-0	.765
Chicago Bears	9-4-1	.692
Brooklyn Dodgers	7-4-1	.636
Providence Steamrollers	6-4-1	.600
Staten Island Stapletons	5-5-2	.500
Chicago Cardinals	5-6-2	.455
Portsmouth Spartans	**5-6-3**	**.455**
Frankford Yellowjackets	4-13-1	.222
Minneapolis Redjackets	1-7-1	.125
Newark Tornadoes	1-10-1	.091

1931 NFL	W-L-T	Pct.
Green Bay Packers	12-2-0	.857
Portsmouth Spartans	**11-3-0**	**.786**
Chicago Bears	8-5-0	.615
Chicago Cardinals	5-4-0	.556
New York Giants	7-6-1	.538
Providence Steamrollers	4-4-3	.500
Staten Island Stapletons	4-6-1	.400
Cleveland Indians	**2-8-0**	**.200**
Brooklyn Dodgers	2-12-0	.143
Frankford Yellowjackets	1-6-1	.143

1932 NFL	W-L-T	Pct.
Chicago Bears*	7-1-6	.875
Green Bay Packers	10-3-1	.769
Portsmouth Spartans*	**6-2-4**	**.750**
Boston Braves	4-4-2	.500
New York Giants	4-6-2	.400
Brooklyn Dodgers	3-9-0	.250
Chicago Cardinals	2-6-2	.250
Staten Island Stapletons	2-7-3	.222

*Bears and Spartans finished the regular season tied for first place. Bears won playoff game 9-0, which counted in the standings.

1933 NFL Eastern Division	W-L-T	Pct.	Western Division	W-L-T	
New York Giants	11-3-0	.786	Chicago Bears	10-2-1	.833
Brooklyn Dodgers	5-4-1	.556	**Portsmouth Spartans**	**6-5-0**	**.545**
Boston Redskins	5-5-2	.500	Green Bay Packers	5-7-1	.417
Philadelphia Eagles	3-5-1	.375	**Cincinnati Reds**	**3-6-1**	**.333**
Pittsburgh Pirates	3-6-2	.333	Chicago Cardinals	1-9-1	.100

COMPLETE STANDINGS

NFL Championship Game:
Bears—23 Giants—21

1934 NFL Eastern Division	W-L-T	Pct	Western Division	W-L-T	Pct.
New York Giants	8-5-0	.615	Chicago Bears	13-0-0	1.000
Boston Redskins	6-6-0	.500	Detroit Lions	10-3-0	.769
Brooklyn Dodgers	4-7-0	.364	Green Bay Packers	7-6-0	.538
Philadelphia Eagles	4-7-0	.364	Chicago Cardinals	5-6-0	.455
Pittsburgh Pirates	2-10-0	.167	St. Louis Gunners	1-2-0	.333
			Cincinnati Reds	0-8-0	.000

NFL Championship Game:
Giants—30 Bears—13

1935 NFL Eastern Division	W-L-T	Pct	Western Division	W-L-T	Pct.
New York Giants	9-3-0	.750	Detroit Lions	7-3-2	.700
Brooklyn Dodgers	5-6-1	.455	Green Bay Packers	8-4-0	.667
Pittsburgh Pirates	4-8-0	.333	Chicago Bears	6-4-2	.600
*Boston Redskins	2-8-1	.200	Chicago Cardinals	6-4-2	.600
*Philadelphia Eagles	2-9-0	.182			

*One game between
Boston and Philadelphia
was cancelled.

NFL Championship Game:
Lions—26 Giants—7

Team Rosters

1920 Akron Pros (8-0-3, 1st)
Head coach—Elgie Tobin
Home field—League Park

Roster		Results		
Player—Position	Date	Opponent	Score	Crowd
Russ Bailey—C	3 Oct	Wheeling*	43-0 W	4,000
Scotty Bierce—E	10 Oct	Columbus Panhandles	37-0 W	1,500
Matt Brown—HB	17 Oct	Cincinnati Celts*	13-0 W	2,000
Alf Cobb—G	24 Oct	Cleveland Tigers	7-0 W	5,000
Tuffy Conn—WB	31 Oct	at Canton Bulldogs	10-0 W	10,000
Charlie Copley—T	14 Nov	at Cleveland Tigers	7-7 T	8,000
Ken Crawford—FB	21 Nov	Dayton Triangles	13-0 W	3,700
Budge Garrett—G	25 Nov	Canton Bulldogs	7-0 W	6,500
Harry Harris—BB	28 Nov	at Dayton Triangles	14-0 W	5,000
Tommy Holleran—BB	5 Dec	at Buffalo All-Americans	0-0 T	3,000
Pike Johnson—T	12 Dec	at Decatur Staleys	0-0 T	12,000
Rip King—TB				
Frank McCormick—FB		*nonleague team		
Buck Miles—FB				
Frank Moran—T				
Bob Nash—E				
Al Nesser—E				
Al Pierotti—C				
Fritz Pollard—WB				
Bill Preston—T				
Fred Sweetland—WB				
Elgie Tobin—BB				
Tommy Tomlin—G				

1920 Canton Bulldogs (7-4-2, 8th)

Head coach—Jim Thorpe
Home field—Lakeside Park

Roster		Results		
Player—Position	Date	Opponent	Score	Crowd
Cub Buck—T	3 Oct	Pitcairn (PA) Quakers*	48-0 W	n/a
Pete Calac—FB	10 Oct	Toledo Maroons*	42-0 W	n/a
Bunny Corcoran—E	17 Oct	Cleveland Tigers	7-0 W	7,000
Harrie Dadmun—G	24 Oct	at Dayton Triangles	20-20 T	5,000
Cap Edwards—G	31 Oct	Akron Pros	0-10 L	10,000
Al Feeney—C	7 Nov	at Cleveland Tigers	18-0 W	8,000
Birdie Gardner—T	14 Nov	Chicago Tigers	21-0 W	8,000
Johnny Gilroy—BB	21 Nov	at Buffalo All-Americans	3-0 W	15,000
Tom Gormley—G	25 Nov	at Akron Pros	0-7 L	6,500
Larry Green—E	4 Dec	at Buffalo All-Americans	3-7 L	10,000
Tex Grigg—BB	5 Dec	at Washington (CT) Glee Club*	0-0 T	3,000
Joe Guyon—WB	11 Dec	at Union (PA) A.A.*	7-13 L	17,000
Doc Haggerty—G	18 Dec	at Richmond (VA) As*	39-0 W	n/a
Art Haley—WB				
Johnny Hendren—TB				
Pete Henry—T				
Bob Higgins—E		*nonleague team		
John Kellison—G				
Bull Lowe—E				
Buck MacDonald—BB				
Al Maginnes—C				
Ike Martin—WB				
Ralph Meadow—E				
Joe Murphy—G				
Dan O'Connor—G				
Larry Petty—G				
Lou Smyth—TB				
Dutch Speck—G				
Jim Thorpe—HB				
Tom Whelan—E				

1920 Cleveland Tigers (2-4-2, 10th)

Head coaches—Al Pierotti, Stan Cofall
Home field—League Park

Roster		Results		
Player—Position	Date	Opponent	Score	Crowd
Bert Baston—E	10 Oct	at Dayton Triangles	0-0 T	n/a
Harry Baujan—E	17 Oct	at Canton Bulldogs	0-7 L	7,000
George Brickley—TB	24 Oct	at Akron Pros	0-7 L	5,000
Jim Bryant—BB	31 Oct	Columbus Panhandles	7-0 W	5,000
Stan Cofall—TB	7 Nov	Canton Bulldogs	0-18 L	8,000
Tuffy Conn—WB	14 Nov	Akron Pros	7-7 T	8,000
Carl Cramer—FB	21 Nov	Toledo Maroons*	14-0 W	n/a
Mark Devlin—BB	28 Nov	at Buffalo All-Americans	0-7 L	5,000
Dinger Doane—FB				
Moon Ducote—WB		*nonleague team		
Johnny Gilroy—BB				
Tom Gormley—G				
Doc Haggerty—G				
Sandy Hastings—WB				
Pat Herron—E				
George Kerr—T				
Phil Marshall—E				
Joe Mattern—TB				
Ed O'Hearn—G				
Jack O'Hearn—WB				
Red Pearlman—T				
Leo Petree—FB				
Al Pierotti—C				
Frank Rydzewski—C				
Herb Sies—T				
Butch Spagna—T				
Jake Stahl—G				
Tiny Thornhill—T				
Ray Trowbridge—E				
Al Wesbecher—C				

COMPLETE STANDINGS

1920 Columbus Panhandles (2-6-2, 13th)

Head coach—Ted Nesser
Home field—Neil Park

Roster   **Results**

Player—Position	Date	Opponent	Score		Crowd
Beckwith—TB	3 Oct	at Dayton Triangles	0-14	L	4,000
Hi Brigham—G	10 Oct	at Akron Pros	0-37	L	1,500
John Davis—FB	17 Oct	at Ft. Wayne Friars*	0-14	L	5,000
Charlie Essman—G	24 Oct	at Detroit Heralds	0-6	L	n/a
Jim Flower—E	31 Oct	at Cleveland Tigers	0-7	L	5,000
Hal Gaulke—BB	7 Nov	at Zanesville Mark Grays*	10-0	W	n/a
Babe Houck—G	14 Nov	at Buffalo All-Americans	7-43	L	9,000
Oscar Kuehner—T	21 Nov	at Zanesville Mark Grays*	0-0	T	n/a
Frank Lone Star—G	25 Nov	at Elyria As*	0-0	T	n/a
Wilkie Moody—WB	5 Dec	Columbus Pirates*	24-0	W	2,000
Joe Mulbarger—T					
Frank Nesser—FB					
Phil Nesser—G					
Ted Nesser—T		*nonleague team			
Dwight Peabody—E					
Homer Ruh—E					
John Schneider—WB					
Lee Snoots—TB					
Wil Waite—C					
Oscar Wolford—G					
Howard Yerges—TB					

1920 Dayton Triangles (5-2-2, 6th)

Head coach—Bud Talbott
Home field—Triangle Park

Roster		Results		
Player—Position	**Date**	**Opponent**	**Score**	**Crowd**
Dick Abrell—BB	3 Oct	Columbus Panhandles	14-0 W	4,000
Francis Bacon—WB	10 Oct	Cleveland Tigers	0-0 T	n/a
Max Broadhurst—T	17 Oct	Hammond Pros	44-0 W	2,000
Bill Clark—G	24 Oct	Canton Bulldogs	20-20 T	5,000
Harry Cutler—T	31 Oct	Cincinnati Celts*	23-7 W	n/a
Doc Davis—G	14 Nov	at Rock Island Independents	21-0 W	n/a
Larry Dellinger—G	21 Nov	at Akron Pros	0-13 L	3,700
Guy Early—G	25 Nov	Detroit Heralds	28-0 W	n/a
Lee Fenner—E	28 Nov	Akron Pros	0-14 L	5,000
Russ Hathaway—T				
Earl Hauser—T				
Chuck Helvie—E		*nonleague team		
Hobby Kinderdine—C				
Pesty Lentz—FB				
Al Mahrt—BB				
Lou Partlow—FB				
Dave Reese—E				
George Roudebush—TB				
Norn Sacksteder—TB				
Ed Sauer—T				
Fritz Slackford—FB				

COMPLETE STANDINGS

1921 Akron Pros (8-3-1, 3rd)

Head coaches—Elgie Tobin, Fritz Pollard
Home field—League Park

Roster		Results			
Player—Position	Date	Opponent	Score		Crowd
Russ Bailey—C	25 Sep	Columbus Panhandles	14-0	W	2,000
Marty Beck—FB	2 Oct	Cincinnati Celts	41-0	W	2,500
Scotty Bierce—E	9 Oct	at Chicago Cardinals	23-0	W	6,000
Alf Cobb—G	16 Oct	at Detroit Tigers	20-0	W	6,000
Charlie Copley—T	23 Oct	at Canton Bulldogs	3-0	W	8,000
Bunny Corcoran—E	30 Oct	Rochester Jeffersons	19-0	W	4,000
Carl Cramer—BB	6 Nov	at Columbus Panhandles	21-0	W	4,100
Jim Flower—E	13 Nov	at Buffalo All-Americans	0-0	T	4,600
Bruno Haas—BB	20 Nov	at Dayton Triangles	0-3	L	n/a
Pike Johnson—T	24 Nov	Canton Bulldogs	0-14	L	4,000
Marshall Jones—WB	3 Dec	at Buffalo All-Americans	0-14	L	n/a
Rip King—TB	4 Dec	at Chicago Cardinals	7-0	W	3,500
Frank McCormick—FB					
Al Nesser—G					
Fritz Pollard—WB					
Roy Ratekin—E					
Jack Reed—G					
Paul Robeson—E					
Paul Sheeks—BB					
Elgie Tobin—BB					
Leo Tobin—G					
Tommy Tomlin—G					

1921 Canton Bulldogs (5-2-3, 4th)

Head coach—Cap Edwards
Home field—Lakeside Park

Roster		Results		
Player—Position	Date	Opponent	Score	Crowd
Bird Carroll—E	9 Oct	Hammond Pros	7-7 T	n/a
Larry Convover—C	16 Oct	at Dayton Triangles	14-14 T	n/a
Cap Edwards—G	23 Oct	Akron Pros	0-3 L	8,000
Guil Falcon—FB	6 Nov	Dayton Triangles	14-0 W	n/a
Al Feeney—C	13 Nov	at Cleveland Indians	7-0 W	3,500
Red Griffiths—G	20 Nov	at Buffalo All-Americans	7-7 T	3,500
Tex Grigg—TB	24 Nov	at Akron Pros	14-0 W	4,000
Pete Henry—T	27 Nov	at Washington Senators	15-0 W	4,000
Bob Higgins—E	11 Dec	at Chicago Staleys	0-10 L	3,000
John Kellison—G	18 Dec	at Washington Senators	28-14 W	6,000
Herb Kempton—BB				
Glenn Killinger—TB				
Jim Laird—FB				
Jim Morrow—WB				
Duke Osborn—G				
Harry Robb—BB				
Ed Sauer—G				
Fritz Slackford—WB				
Marv Smith—TB				
Lou Smyth—TB				
Dutch Speck—G				
Red Steele—E				
Charlie Way—WB				
Belf West—T				
Inky Williams—E				
Swede Youngstrom—G				

1921 Cincinnati Celts (1-3, 13th)

Head coach—Mel Doherty
Home field—None

Roster		Results		
Player—Position	Date	Opponent	Score	Crowd
Ferris Beekley—G	2 Oct	at Akron Pros	0-41 L	2,500
Ken Crawford—BB	16 Oct	at Muncie Flyers	14-0 W	n/a
Dane Dastillung—G	23 Oct	at Cleveland Indians	0-28 L	n/a
Fred Day—T	27 Nov	at Evansville Crimson Giants	0-48 L	n/a
Mel Doherty—C				
Guy Early—G				
Earl Hauser—E				
Shiner Knab—WB				
Art Lewis—T				
Lynch—G				
Frank McCormick—FB				
Tommy McMahon—FB				
Tom Melvin—E				
George Munns—TB				
Ohmer—WB				
Henry Orth—G				
Walt Schupp—T				
Dave Thompson—WB				
Pete Volz—E				

1921 Cleveland Indians (3-5, 11th)

Head coach—Jim Thorpe
Home field—League Park

Roster		Results		
Player—Position	Date	Opponent	Score	Crowd
Harry Baujan—E	16 Oct	Columbus Panhandles	35-9 W	3,000
Phil Bower—BB	23 Oct	Cincinnati Celts	28-0 W	n/a
Ed Brawley—G	30 Oct	at Dayton Triangles	2-3 L	4,000
Pete Calac—FB	6 Nov	at Buffalo All-Americans	6-10 L	3,000
Bunny Corcoran—E	13 Nov	Canton Bulldogs	0-7 L	3,500
Milt Ghee—BB	20 Nov	at Chicago Staleys	7-22 L	10,000
Joe Guyon—TB	3 Dec	at Brickley New York Giants	17-0 W	3,000
Bruno Haas—WB	11 Dec	at Washington Senators	0-7 L	5,000
Johnny Hendren—FB				
Bull Lowe—T				
Moore—T				
Joe Murphy—G				
Dan O'Connor—T				
Patterson—BB				
Red Pearlman—G				
Jake Stahl—G				
George Tandy—C				
Jim Thorpe—TB				
Ralph Waldsmith—C				
Tom Whelan—E				

COMPLETE STANDINGS

1921 Columbus Panhandles (1-8, 17th)

Head coach—Ted Nesser
Home field—Neil Park

Roster		Results		
Player—Position	Date	Opponent	Score	Crowd
Harry Bliss—BB	25 Sep	at Akron Pros	0-14 L	2,000
Hal Gaulke—BB	2 Oct	at Dayton Triangles	13-42 L	n/a
Morris Glassman—E	9 Oct	at Buffalo All-Americans	0-38 L	n/a
Ted Hopkins—E	16 Oct	at Cleveland Indians	9-35 L	3,000
Babe Houck—G	23 Oct	at Chicago Cardinals	6-17 L	6,000
Oscar Kuehner—T	30 Oct	at Minneapolis Marines	0-28 L	n/a
Joe Mulbarger—T	6 Nov	Akron Pros	0-21 L	4,000
Ted Murtha—G	20 Nov	at Rochester Jeffersons	13-27 L	2,500
Charlie Nesser—TB	4 Dec	at Louisville Brecks	6-0 W	n/a
Frank Nesser—FB				
Fred Nesser—T				
John Nesser—G				
Phil Nesser—T				
Ted Nesser—C				
Walt Rogers—WB				
Emmett Ruh—WB				
Homer Ruh—E				
Al Shook—G				
Will Waite—G				
Oscar Wolford—G				

1921 Dayton Triangles (4-4-1, 8th)

Head coach—Nelson Talbot
Home field—Triangle Park

Roster		Results		
Player—Position	Date	Opponent	Score	Crowd
Faye Abbott—BB	2 Oct	Columbus Panhandles	42-13 W	n/a
Francis Bacon—TB	9 Oct	at Detroit Tigers	7-10 L	n/a
Larry Dellinger—G	16 Oct	Canton Bulldogs	14-14 T	n/a
Lee Fenner—E	23 Oct	at Chicago Staleys	0-7 L	8,000
Art Haley—TB	30 Oct	Cleveland Indians	3-2 W	4,000
Russ Hathaway—T	6 Nov	at Canton Bulldogs	0-14 L	n/a
Hobby Kinderdine—C	13 Nov	Detroit Tigers	27-0 W	n/a
Al Mahrt—BB	20 Nov	Akron Pros	3-0 W	n/a
John Miller—FB	27 Nov	at Buffalo All-Americans	0-7 L	n/a
Wilkie Moody—WB				
Lou Partlow—FB				
Gus Redman—WB				
Dave Reese—E				
George Roudebush—FB				
Nelson Rupp—WB				
Art Sampson—G				
Ed Sauer—T				
Herb Sies—G				
Frank Sillin—WB				
Jake Stahl—T				
Dutch Thiele—E				
Glenn Tidd—C				
Chalmers Tschappatt—T				

1922 Akron Pros (3-5-2, 10th)

Head coach—Ed "Untz" Brewer
Home field—Elks Field

Roster		Results			
Player—Position	Date	Opponent	Score		Crowd
Marty Beck—WB	1 Oct	Columbus Panhandles	36-0	W	3,000
Scotty Bierce—E	12 Oct	Rochester Jeffersons	13-13	T	2,000
Untz Brewer—WB	22 Oct	Canton Bulldogs	0-22	L	7,000
Charlie Copley—T	29 Oct	Oorang Indians	62-0	W	3,000
Bunny Corcoran—E	5 Nov	Hammond Pros	22-0	W	n/a
Carl Cramer—FB	12 Nov	at Chicago Cardinals	0-7	L	2,000
Red Daum—E	19 Nov	at Buffalo All-Americans	3-3	T	4,000
Jim Flower—C	26 Nov	at Chicago Bears	10-20	L	6,000
Al Jolley—T	30 Nov	at Canton Bulldogs	0-14	L	3,500
Rip King—TB	3 Dec	at Buffalo All-Americans	0-16	L	n/a
Walt Kreinheder—C					
Walt LeJeune—G					
Leo McCausland—G					
Joe Mills—WB					
Ray Neal—G					
Al Nesser—G					
Ed Sauer—T					
Paul Sheeks—BB					
Bob Spiers—T					
Cliff Steele—BB					
Tillie Voss—E					

1922 Canton Bulldogs (10-0-2, 1st)

Head coach—Guy Chamberlin
Home field—Lakeside Park

Roster		Results			
Player—Position	Date	Opponent	Score		Crowd
Don Batchelor—T	1 Oct	Louisville Brecks	38-0	W	3,000
Arda Bowser—FB	8 Oct	at Dayton Triangles	0-0	T	3,000
Bird Carroll—E	15 Oct	Oorang Indians	14-0	W	7,000
Guy Chamberlin—E	22 Oct	at Akron Pros	22-0	W	7,000
Doc Elliott—FB	29 Oct	at Chicago Bears	7-6	W	10,000
Tex Grigg—WB	5 Nov	Toledo Maroons	0-0	T	n/a
Russ Hathaway—T	12 Nov	Buffalo All-Americans	3-0	W	n/a
Pete Henry—T	19 Nov	at Chicago Cardinals	7-0	W	7,500
Jim Kendrick—E	26 Nov	Chicago Cardinals	20-3	W	2,500
Link Lyman—T	30 Nov	Akron Pros	14-0	W	3,500
Johnny McQuade—WB	3 Dec	Milwaukee Badgers	40-6	W	3,000
Candy Miller—FB	10 Dec	at Toledo Maroons	19-0	W	5,000
William Murrah—C					
Duke Osborn—G					
Harry Robb—WB					
Wooky Roberts—BB					
Norb Sacksteder—TB					
Ed Shaw—FB					
Lou Smyth—TB					
Dutch Speck—C					
Tarzan Taylor—G					
Ralph Waldsmith—G					

COMPLETE STANDINGS

1922 Columbus Panhandles (0-8, 18th)

Head coach—Herb Dell
Home field—Neil Park

Roster		Results		
Player—Position	Date	Opponent	Score	Crowd
Burl Atcheson—E	1 Oct	at Akron Pros	0-36 L	3,000
Jack Beckett—T	8 Oct	at Oorang Indians	6-20 L	1,200
Chuck Carney—T	15 Oct	at Buffalo All-Americans	0-19 L	n/a
Gene Carroll—E	29 Oct	at Chicago Cardinals	6-37 L	5,000
John Conley—G	5 Nov	at Green Bay Packers	0-3 L	2,000
Doc Davis—G	11 Nov	at Racine Legion	0-34 L	4,000
Hal Gaulke—BB	26 Nov	at Toledo Maroons	6-7 L	1,700
Morris Glassman—E	30 Nov	Oorang Indians	6-18 L	3,000
Andy Gump—G				
Ted Hopkins—E				
Bob Karch—T				
Earl Kreiger—E				
Joe Mulbarger—T				
Frank Nesser—G				
Bob Rapp—WB				
Walt Rogers—FB				
Emmett Ruh—WB				
Homer Ruh—E				
Pete Schultz—FB				
Lee Snoots—TB				
Mark Stevenson—G				
Don Wiper—BB				
Oscar Wolford—C				
Paul Ziegler—FB				

APPENDIX

1922 Dayton Triangles (4-3-1, 7th)

Head coach—Carl Storck
Home field—Triangle Park

Roster					
Player—Position	**Date**	**Opponent**	**Score**		**Crowd**
Faye Abbott—BB	1 Oct	Oorang Indians	36-0	W	n/a
Francis Bacon—TB	8 Oct	Canton Bulldogs	0-0	T	3,000
Bobby Berns—G	15 Oct	Minneapolis Marines	17-0	W	n/a
Larry Dellinger—G	22 Oct	Hammond Pros	20-0	W	n/a
Lee Fenner—E	29 Oct	Buffalo All-Americans	0-7	L	5,000
Bruno Haas—G	5 Nov	at Chicago Bears	0-9	L	n/a
Russ Hathaway—T	12 Nov	at Rock Island Independents	0-43	L	n/a
Ken Huffine—FB	3 Dec	at Chicago Cardinals	7-3	W	n/a
Hobby Kinderdine—C					
Al Mahrt—BB					
Tip O'Neill—WB					
Lou Partlow—FB					
Gus Redman—TB					
Dave Reese—E					
Ed Sauer—T					
Gherb Sies—G					
Dutch Thiele—E					
Glenn Tidd—C					
Jiggs Ullery—WB					

1922 Oorang Indians (3-6, 12th)

Head coach—Jim Thorpe
Home field—Lincoln Park (Marion, Ohio)

Roster		Results		
Player—Position	Date	Opponent	Score	Crowd
Reggie Attache—WB	1 Oct	at Dayton Triangles	0-36 L	n/a
Big Bear—E	8 Oct	Columbus Panhandles	20-6 W	1,200
E. Bobadash—E	15 Oct	at Canton Bulldogs	0-14 L	7,000
Lo Boutwell—BB	29 Oct	at Akron Pros	0-62 L	3,000
Fred Broker—T	5 Nov	at Minneapolis Marines	6-13 L	4,000
Elmer Busch—G	12 Nov	at Chicago Bears	6-33 L	n/a
Pete Calac—E	19 Nov	at Milwaukee Badgers	0-13 L	6,500
Dick Deer Slayer—E	26 Nov	at Buffalo All-Americans	19-7 W	n/a
Xavier Downwind—C	30 Nov	at Columbus Panhandles	18-6 W	3,000
Eagle Feather—FB				
Joe Guyon—TB				
Bob Hill—G				
Horatio Jones—E				
Nick Lassa—T				
Joe Little Twig—E				
Ted Lone Wolf—G				
Ed Nason—E				
Stillwell Sanooke—E				
Ted St. Germaine—T				
Jim Thorpe—TB				
Baptise Thunder—T				
War Eagle—T				
Bill Winneshick—C				

1922 Toledo Maroons (5-2-2, 4th)

Head coach—Guil Falcon
Home field—Swayne Field

Roster		Results		
Player—Position	Date	Opponent	Score	Crowd
Dunc Annan—WB	1 Oct	Evansville Crimson Giants	15-0 W	2,000
Al Burgin—G	8 Oct	Milwaukee Badgers	12-12 T	2,000
Marty Conrad—C	15 Oct	Hammond Pros	14-0 W	2,000
Cap Edwards—G	22 Oct	at Racine Legion	7-0 W	3,500
Guil Falcon—FB	29 Oct	Louisville Brecks	39-0 W	2,500
Hippo Gozdowski—FB	5 Nov	at Canton Bulldogs	0-0 T	n/a
Tom Holleran—BB	26 Nov	Columbus Panhandles	7-6 W	1,700
Steamer Horning—T	3 Dec	at Chicago Bears	0-22 L	6,000
Reno Jones—G	10 Dec	Canton Bulldogs	0-19 L	5,000
John Kellison—T				
Tex Kelly—G				
Jim Kendrick—TB				
Gus King—E				
Truck Myers—E				
Chuck O'Neil—FB				
Dwight Peabody—E				
Leo Petree—FB				
Bob Phelan—BB				
Red Roberts—TB				
Tubby Rousch—WB				
Buck Saunders—BB				
Jimmy Simpson—BB				
Herb Stein—G				
Russ Stein—T				
John Tanner—WB				
Festus Tierney—G				
Rat Watson—TB				
Mac White—E				

1923 Akron Pros (1-6, 17th)

Head coaches—Dutch Hendrian, Wayne Brenkert
Home field—Wooster Ave. Stadium

Roster			Results		
Player—Position	Date	Opponent		Score	Crowd
Francis Bacon—WB	30 Sep	at Duluth Kelleys	7-10	L	3,000
Wayne Brenkert—WB	7 Oct	at Buffalo All-Americans	0-9	L	n/a
George Brown—T	14 Oct	at Chicago Cardinals	0-19	L	n/a
Carl Cramer—FB	21 Oct	at Racine Legion	7-9	L	n/a
Red Daum—E	28 Oct	at Canton Bulldogs	3-7	L	2,500
Bill Edgar—G	11 Nov	at Chicago Bears	6-20	L	4,000
Jim Flower—T	29 Nov	Buffalo All-Americans	2-0	W	1,700
Art Haley—WB					
Isham Hardy—G					
Dutch Hendrian—BB					
Walt LeJeune—G					
Grover Malone—E					
Al Michaels—TB					
Joe Mills—C					
Al Nesser—E					
Red Roberts—E					
Lee Scott—G					
Ed Shaw—HB					
Hugh Sprinkle—T					
Charlie Stewart—G					
Dutch Wallace—G					
Wilson—T					

1923 Canton Bulldogs (11-0-1, 1st)

Head coach—Guy Chamberlin
Home field—Lakeside Park

Roster		Results		
Player—Position	Date	Opponent	Score	Crowd
Bird Carroll—E	30 Sep	Hammond Pros	17-0 W	5,000
Guy Chamberlin—E	7 Oct	Louisville Brecks	37-0 W	n/a
Rudy Comstock—G	14 Oct	Dayton Triangles	30-0 W	n/a
Larry Conover—C	21 Oct	at Chicago Bears	6-0 W	n/a
Doc Elliott—FB	28 Oct	Akron Pros	7-3 W	2,500
Tex Grigg—WB	4 Nov	at Chicago Cardinals	7-3 W	6,000
Dutch Hendrian—WB	11 Nov	at Buffalo All-Americans	3-3 T	10,000
Pete Henry—T	18 Nov	Oorang Indians	41-0 W	5,000
Ben Jones—FB	25 Nov	at Cleveland Indians	46-10 W	17,000
Link Lyman—T	29 Nov	Toledo Maroons	28-0 W	3,000
Vern Mullen—E	2 Dec	Buffalo All-Americans	14-0 W	4,000
Duke Osborn—G	9 Dec	at Columbus Tigers	10-0 W	1,700
Harry Robb—BB				
Wooky Roberts—BB				
Ben Roderick—WB				
Ben Shaw—G				
Russ Smith—G				
Lou Smyth—TB				
Dutch Speck—C				
Joe Williams—G				

1923 Cleveland Indians (3-1-3, 5th)

Head coach—Cap Edwards
Home field—League Park

Roster		Results		
Player—Position	Date	Opponent	Score	Crowd
Hunk Anderson—G	7 Oct	at Rock Island Independents	0-0 T	3,500
Pete Bahan—BB	21 Oct	St. Louis All-Stars	6-0 W	7,000
Scotty Bierce—E	28 Oct	Oorang Indians	27-0 W	n/a
Arda Bowser—FB	4 Nov	at Buffalo All-Americans	0-0 T	3,000
Frank Civiletto—WB	11 Nov	Dayton Triangles	0-0 T	11,000
Hal Ebersole—G	18 Nov	Columbus Tigers	9-3 W	6,000
Deke Edler—WB	25 Nov	Canton Bulldogs	10-46 L	17,000
Cap Edwards—T				
Frank Garden—E				
Charlie Guy—C				
Iolas Huffman—T				
Ed Johns—G				
Stan Keck—T				
Johnny Kyle—FB				
Bo McMillin—WB				
Truck Myers—E				
Lou Partlow—FB				
Doug Roby—TB				
Rudy Rosatti—T				
Joe Setron—G				
Pete Stinchcomb—WB				
John Tanner—BB				
Ralph Vince—G				
Sol Weinberg—TB				
Dick Wolf—FB				
Joe Work—E				

APPENDIX

1923 Columbus Tigers (5-4-1, 9th)

Head coaches—Gus Tebell, Pete Stinchcomb
Home field—Neil Park

Roster		Results		
Player—Position	Date	Opponent	Score	Crowd
Elliott Bonowitz—BB	30 Sep	at Dayton Triangles	6-7 L	6,000
Paul Goebel—E	7 Oct	at Milwaukee Badgers	0-0 T	2,000
Gus Goetz—T	14 Oct	Buffalo All-Americans	0-3 L	3,500
Ray Hanson—G	21 Oct	Louisville Brecks	34-0 W	2,500
Jack Heldt—C	28 Oct	at Toledo Maroons	3-0 W	5,000
Wilmer Isabel—FB	11 Nov	Toledo Maroons	16-0 W	3,500
Joe Mulbarger—T	18 Nov	at Cleveland Indians	3-9 L	6,000
Andy Nemecek—G	25 Nov	Oorang Indians	27-3 W	n/a
Bill Passuelo—G	2 Dec	Dayton Triangles	30-3 W	3,000
Harry Randolph—BB	9 Dec	Canton Bulldogs	0-10 L	1,700
Bob Rapp—WB				
Homer Ruh—E				
Jack Sack—G				
Lee Snoots—BB				
Gus Sonnenberg—T				
Pete Stinchcomb—WB				
Gus Tebell—E				
Red Weaver—C				
Sonny Winters—TB				

1923 Dayton Triangles (1-6-1, 16th)

Head coach—Carl Storck
Home field—Triangle Park

Roster		Results		
Player—Position	Date	Opponent	Score	Crowd
Faye Abbott—BB	30 Sep	Columbus Tigers	7-6 W	6,000
Francis Bacon—WB	7 Oct	at Hammond Pros	0-7 L	n/a
John Beasley—G	14 Oct	at Canton Bulldogs	0-30 L	n/a
Bobby Berns—G	21 Oct	at Toledo Maroons	3-6 L	3,000
Earl Burgner—BB	28 Oct	at Chicago Cardinals	3-13 L	5,000
Ken Crawford—FB	11 Nov	at Cleveland Indians	0-0 T	11,000
Larry Dellinger—G	18 Nov	at Buffalo All-Americans	0-3 L	3,500
Lee Fenner—E	2 Dec	at Columbus Tigers	3-30 L	3,000
Russ Hathaway—T				
Ken Huffine—FB				
Al Jolley—G				
Hobby Kinderdine—C				
Walt Kinderdine—FB				
Lou Partlow—TB				
Dave Reese—E				
Ed Sauer—T				
Dutch Thiele—E				
Glenn Tidd—G				

1923 Oorang Indians (1-10, 18th)

Head coach—Jim Thorpe
Home field—Lincoln Park (Marion, Ohio)

Roster		Results		
Player—Position	Date	Opponent	Score	Crowd
Arrowhead—E	30 Sep	at Milwaukee Badgers	2-13 L	4,000
Napoleon Barrel—C	7 Oct	at Toledo Maroons	0-7 L	5,000
Big Bear—T	14 Oct	at Minneapolis Marines	0-23 L	4,000
Peter Black Bear—E	21 Oct	at Buffalo All-Americans	0-57 L	n/a
Lo Boutwell—BB	28 Oct	at Cleveland Indians	0-27 L	n/a
Ted Buffalo—T	4 Nov	at Chicago Bears	0-26 L	1,000
Pete Calac—FB	11 Nov	at St. Louis All-Stars	7-14 L	5,000
Xavier Downwind—G	18 Nov	at Canton Bulldogs	0-41 L	5,000
Eagle Feather—FB	25 Nov	at Columbus Tigers	3-27 L	n/a
Gray Horse—WB	2 Dec	at Chicago Cardinals	19-22 L	1,200
Joe Guyon—TB	9 Dec	at Louisville Brecks	19-0 W	1,200
Al Jolley—T				
Nick Lassa—C				
Chim Lingrel—WB				
Joe Little Twig—E				
Ted Lone Wolf—G				
Emmett McLemore—BB				
Ed Nason—E				
Bill Newashe—T				
Joe Pappio—E				
Stan Powell—G				
Jack Thorpe—G				
Jim Thorpe—TB				
Woodchuck Welmas—E				

1923 Toledo Maroons (3-3-2, 11th)

Head coach—Guil Falcon
Home field—Armory Park

Roster		Results			
Player—Position	Date	Opponent	Score		Crowd
Don Batchelor—T	30 Sep	at Racine Legion	7-7	T	3,500
Marty Conrad—C	7 Oct	Oorang Indians	7-0	W	5,000
Guil Falcon—FB	21 Oct	Dayton Triangles	6-3	W	3,000
France Fitzgerald—BB	28 Oct	Columbus Tigers	0-3	L	5,000
Joe Gillis—G	11 Nov	at Columbus Tigers	0-16	L	3,500
Cowboy Hill—TB	24 Nov	at Rochester Jeffersons	12-6	W	n/a
Steamer Horning—T	25 Nov	at Buffalo All-Americans	3-3	T	n/a
Ben Hunt—T	29 Nov	at Canton Bulldogs	0-28	L	3,000
Cliff Jetmore—WB					
Jerry Jones—G					
Heinie Kirkgard—WB					
Dutch Lauer—WB					
Tom McNamara—G					
Chuck O'Neil—E					
Si Seyfrit—E					
Dutch Strauss—FB					
Tillie Voss—T					
Rat Watson—BB					
Mac White—E					

1924 Akron Pros (2-6, 13th)

Head coach—Wayne Brenkert
Home field—General (Tire) Field

Roster		Results			
Player—Position	Date	Opponent	Score		Crowd
John Barrett—C	5 Oct	at Rochester Jeffersons	3-0	W	1,200
Marty Beck—WB	12 Oct	at Cleveland Bulldogs	14-29	L	n/a
George Berry—G	26 Oct	at Buffalo Bisons	13-17	L	8,000
Wayne Brenkert—BB	1 Nov	at Frankford Yellowjackets	0-23	L	6,000
Sol Butler—WB	2 Nov	at Columbus Tigers	0-30	L	3,000
Carl Cardarelli—C	9 Nov	Cleveland Bulldogs	7-20	L	5,000
Carl Cramer—FB	16 Nov	at Chicago Cardinals	0-13	L	2,500
Red Daum—E	27 Nov	Buffalo Bisons	22-0	W	1,000
Jim Flower—T					
Paul Hogan—WB					
Frank Hogue—BB					
Al Michaels—TB					
Joe Mills—E					
Stan Mills—E					
Al Nesser—G					
Harry Newman—G					
James Robertson—BB					
Walt Sechrist—G					
Dutch Speck—G					
Hugh Sprinkle—T					
Dick Stahlman—T					
Dutch Wallace—G					
Wilson—G					
Giff Zimmerman—WB					

1924 Cleveland Bulldogs (7-1-1, 1st)

Head coach—Guy Chamberlin
Home field—League Park

Roster		Results		
Player—Position	Date	Opponent	Score	Crowd
Chalmers Ault—G	5 Oct	Chicago Bears	16-1 W	n/a
Scotty Bierce—E	11 Oct	at Frankford Yellowjackets	3-3 T	n/a
Hal Burt—G	12 Oct	Akron Pros	29-14 W	n/a
Guy Chamberlin—E	26 Oct	Rochester Jeffersons	59-0 W	5,000
Rudy Comstock—G	2 Nov	Dayton Triangles	35-0 W	n/a
Cap Edwards—T	9 Nov	at Akron Pros	20-7 W	5,000
Doc Elliott—FB	16 Nov	at Chicago Cardinals	0-13 L	2,500
Charlie Honaker—E	23 Nov	Columbus Tigers	7-0 W	n/a
Ben Jones—FB	27 Nov	Milwaukee Badgers	53-10 W	4,000
Jerry Jones—G		(at Canton, Ohio)		
Link Lyman—T				
Stan Muirhead—T				
Dave Noble—WB				
Duke Osborn—C				
Wooky Roberts—BB				
Olin Smith—T				
Russ Smith—G				
John Tanner—FB				
Dick Wolf—WB				
Joe Work—E				
Hoge Workman—TB				

1924 Columbus Tigers (4-4, 10th)

Head coach—Red Weaver
Home field—West Side Athletic Club

Roster		Results		
Player—Position	**Date**	**Opponent**	**Score**	**Crowd**
Earl Duvall—G	5 Oct	at Buffalo Bisons	0-13 L	5,000
Walt Ellis—T	12 Oct	at Rochester Jeffersons	15-7 W	2,000
Paul Goebel—E	18 Oct	at Frankford Yellowjackets	7-23 L	10,000
Neil Halleck—BB	26 Oct	at Dayton Triangles	17-6 W	3,000
Wilmer Isabel—BB	2 Nov	Akron Pros	30-0 W	3,000
Johnnie Layport—G	9 Nov	at Chicago Bears	6-12 L	7,000
Joe Mantell—G	16 Nov	Rochester Jeffersons	16-0 W	2,500
Wilkie Moody—BB	23 Nov	at Cleveland Bulldogs	0-7 L	n/a
Joe Mulbarger—G				
Andy Nemecek—C				
Boni Petcoff—T				
Bob Rapp—WB				
Homer Ruh—E				
Herb Schell—WB				
Herb Stock—BB				
Gus Tebell—E				
Buddy Tynes—FB				
Sonny Winters—TB				
Oscar Wolford—E				

1924 Dayton Triangles (2-6, 14th)

Head coach—Carl Storck
Home field—Triangle Park

Roster		Results		
Player—Position	Date	Opponent	Score	Crowd
Faye Abbott—BB	5 Oct	Frankford Yellowjackets	19-7 W	4,000
Francis Bacon—E	12 Oct	at Buffalo Bisons	7-0 W	6,000
Bobby Berns—G	19 Oct	at Rock Island Independents	0-20 L	4,500
Elliott Bonowitz—G	26 Oct	Columbus Tigers	6-17 L	3,000
Dick Egan—G	2 Nov	at Cleveland Bulldogs	0-35 L	n/a
Dick Faust—G	9 Nov	at Chicago Cardinals	0-23 L	2,500
Lee Fenner—E	16 Nov	at Buffalo Bisons	6-14 L	2,700
Russ Hathaway—T	27 Nov	at Frankford Yellowjackets	7-32 L	15,000
Ken Huffine—FB				
Harry Kinderdine—G				
Hobby Kinderdine—C				
Walt Kinderdine—WB				
Waddy Kuehl—WB				
Armin Mahrt—TB				
Stan Muirhead—G				
Lou Partlow—WB				
Gus Redman—BB				
Ed Sauer—T				
Herb Seis—G				
Glenn Tidd—C				
Inky Williams—E				

1925 Akron Pros (4-2-2, 5th)

Head coach—Scotty Bierce
Home field—General (Tire) Field

Roster		Results		
Player—Position	Date	Opponent	Score	Crowd
Dunc Annan—WB	27 Sep	Cleveland Bulldogs	7-0 W	2,000
John Barrett—C	4 Oct	Kansas City Cowboys	14-7 W	n/a
George Berry—G	11 Oct	at Buffalo Bisons	0-0 T	n/a
Scotty Bierce—E	18 Oct	at Canton Bulldogs	20-3 W	5,000
Frank Bissell—E	25 Oct	at Detroit Panthers	0-0 T	5,400
Russ Blailock—G	1 Nov	Dayton Triangles	17-3 W	2,500
Knute Caldwell—T	7 Nov	at Frankford Yellowjackets	7-17 L	12,000
Chase Clements—T	8 Nov	at Pottsville Maroons	0-21 L	n/a
Marty Conrad—G				
Carl Cramer—FB				
Red Daum—E				
Guil Falcon—FB				
Jim Flower—T				
Fritz Henry—G				
Joe Mills—C				
Al Nesser—G				
Obie Newman—E				
Fanny Niehaus—TB				
Fritz Pollard—TB				
James Robertson—BB				
Dick Stahlman—T				

COMPLETE STANDINGS

1925 Canton Bulldogs (4-4, 11th)

Head coach—Harry Robb
Home field—Lakeside Park

Roster			Results		
Player—Position	Date	Opponent	Score		Crowd
Ray Brenner—WB	27 Sep	Rochester Jeffersons	14-7	W	n/a
Pete Calac—FB	4 Oct	Dayton Triangles	14-0	W	5,000
Bird Carroll—E	10 Oct	at Frankford Yellowjackets	7-12	L	15,000
Rudy Comstock—G	11 Oct	at Pottsville Maroons	0-28	L	n/a
Frank Culver—C	18 Oct	Akron Pros	3-20	L	5,000
Willie Flattery—G	8 Nov	Cleveland Bulldogs	6-0	W	2,000
Wilmer Fleming—WB	22 Nov	Columbus Tigers	6-0	W	n/a
Chick Guarnieri—E	6 Dec	at Cleveland Bulldogs	0-6	L	1,500
Pete Henry—T					
Paul Hogan—TB					
Ben Jones—WB					
Rip Kyle—T					
Link Lyman—T					
Wade McRoberts—C					
Lou Merillat—E					
Reul Redinger—WB					
Harry Robb—BB					
Norb Sacksteder—BB					
Dick Schuster—G					
Dutch Speck—G					
Dutch Strassner—E					
Giff Zimmerman—TB					

1925 Cleveland Bulldogs (5-8-1, 12th)

Head coach—Cap Edwards
Home field—League Park

Roster		Results			
Player—Position	Date	Opponent	Score		Crowd
Chalmers Ault—T	27 Sep	at Akron Pros	0-7	L	2,000
George Baldwin—E	4 Oct	Columbus Tigers	3-0	W	4,000
Herb Bauer—E	11 Oct	Kansas City Cowboys	16-13	W	2,000
Phil Branon—T	18 Oct	at Chicago Bears	0-7	L	n/a
Obie Bristow—TB	1 Nov	at New York Giants	0-19	L	18,000
Karl Broadley—G	8 Nov	at Canton Bulldogs	0-6	L	2,000
Glen Carberry—E	11 Nov	at Detroit Panthers	13-22	L	5,000
Carl Cardarelli—C	21 Nov	at Frankford Yellowjackets	14-0	W	7,000
Chase Clements—T	22 Nov	at Pottsville Maroons	6-24	L	n/a
Alf Cobb—T	26 Nov	Kansas City Cowboys	0-17	L	1,000
Larry Conover—C		at Hartford, CT			
Gus Eckberg—FB	29 Nov	at Providence Steamrollers	7-7	T	7,000
Doc Elliott—FB	6 Dec	Canton Bulldogs	6-0	W	1,500
Frank Garden—E	12 Dec	at Frankford Yellowjackets	3-0	W	7,000
Walt Kreinheder—C	20 Dec	Frankford Yellowjackets	7-13	L	1,000
Rudy Kutler—G					
Ed Loucks—E					
Russ Meredith—T					
Al Michaels—TB					
Truck Myers—T					
Nick Nardacci—TB					
Al Nesser—G					
Dave Noble—WB					
Ray Norton—WB					
Steve Owen—T					
Milt Rehnquist—G					
Wooky Roberts—BB					
Walt Sechrist—T					
Maury Segal—E					
Bob Spiers—T					
Hugh Sprinkle—T					
Gene Stringer—FB					
Paul Suchy—E					
Ralph Vince—G					
Dutch Wallace—G					
Dutch Webber—E					
Inky Williams—E					
Dick Wolf—BB					
Joe Work—E					
Swede Youngstrom—G					

1925 Columbus Tigers (0-9, 20th)

Head coach—Red Weaver
Home field—West Side Athletic Club

Roster		Results		
Player—Position	Date	Opponent	Score	Crowd
Dom Albanese—FB	27 Sep	at Detroit Panthers	0-7 L	3,500
Gale Bullman—E	4 Oct	at Cleveland Bulldogs	0-3 L	4,000
Herb Davis—E	11 Oct	at Chicago Cardinals	9-19 L	n/a
Earl Duvall—G	18 Oct	at Buffalo Bisons	6-17 L	4,500
Ray Eichenlaub—FB	31 Oct	at Frankford Yellowjackets	0-19 L	5,000
Walt Ellis—T	1 Nov	at Pottsville Maroons	0-19 L	3,000
Paul Goebel—E	8 Nov	at New York Giants	0-19 L	4,000
Tom Long—G	22 Nov	at Canton Bulldogs	0-6 L	n/a
Paul Lynch—T	29 Nov	at Chicago Bears	13-14 L	n/a
Wilkie Moody—WB				
Joe Mulbarger—G				
Andy Nemecek—C				
Frank Nesser—FB				
Boni Petcoff—T				
Bob Rapp—BB				
Jim Regan—BB				
George Rohleder—G				
Homer Ruh—E				
Lee Snoots—WB				
Buddy Tynes—WB				

1925 Dayton Triangles (0-7-1, 19th)

Head coach—Carl Storck
Home field—Triangle Park

Roster		Results		
Player—Position	Date	Opponent	Score	Crowd
Faye Abbott—BB	27 Sep	at Rock Island Independents	0-0 T	3,000
Francis Bacon—WB	4 Oct	at Canton Bulldogs	0-14 L	5,000
Elliott Bonowitz—G	18 Oct	at Detroit Panthers	0-6 L	4,132
Dick Dobeleit—WB	24 Oct	at Frankford Yellowjackets	0-3 L	2,000
Clarence Drayer—T	1 Nov	at Akron Pros	3-17 L	2,500
Lee Fenner—E	15 Nov	at Green Bay Packers	0-7 L	3,000
John Gabler—G	22 Nov	at Chicago Cardinals	0-14 L	3,000
Al Graham—G	29 Nov	at New York Giants	0-23 L	18,000
Charlie Guy—G				
Ken Huffine—FB				
Zip Joseph—G				
Hobby Kinderdine—C				
Walt Kinderdine—WB				
Bill Knecht—T				
Johnnie Layport—G				
Armin Mahrt—TB				
Johnny Mahrt—E				
Gene Mayl—E				
Lou Partlow—FB				
Ed Sauer—T				
Russ Young—FB				

1926 Akron Indians (1-4-3, 16th)

Head coaches—Al Nesser, Frank Neid
Home field—General (Tire) Field

Roster	Results				
Player—Position	**Date**	**Opponent**	**Score**		**Crowd**
Dunc Annan—TB	25 Sep	at Frankford Yellowjackets	6-6	T	5,000
Marty Beck—FB	26 Sep	at Buffalo Rangers	0-7	L	2,500
George Berry—C	3 Oct	Hammond Pros	17-0	W	n/a
Frank Bissell—E	10 Oct	Canton Bulldogs	0-0	T	2,500
Knute Caldwell—T	24 Oct	at Detroit Panthers	0-25	L	n/a
Alvro Casey—T	31 Oct	at Chicago Bears	0-17	L	6,500
Ralph Chase—T	7 Nov	at Pottsville Maroons	0-34	L	n/a
Carl Cramer—FB	25 Nov	at Canton Bulldogs	0-0	T	n/a
Red Daum—E					
Hal Griggs—BB					
Isham Hardy—G					
Joe Little Twig—E					
Nat McCombs—G					
Joe Mills—C					
Al Nesser—G					
Obie Newman—WB					
Fritz Pollard—TB					
George Rohleder—T					
Red Seidelson—G					
Rube Ursella—WB					
Dutch Wallace—G					
Hal Wendler—BB					

1926 Canton Bulldogs (1-9-3, 20th)

Head coaches—Pete Henry, Harry Robb
Home field—Lakeside Park

Roster		Results			
Player—Position	Date	Opponent	Score		Crowd
Sam Babcock—WB	26 Sep	Columbus Tigers	2-14	L	2,500
Sol Butler—FB	3 Oct	Louisville Colonels	13-0	W	3,000
Pete Calac—FB	10 Oct	at Akron Indians	0-0	T	2,500
Hook Comber—FB	17 Oct	Los Angeles Buccaneers	13-16	L	5,000
Art Deibel—T	23 Oct	at Frankford Yellowjackets	0-17	L	4,000
Willie Flattery—G	31 Oct	at Detroit Panthers	0-6	L	n/a
Pete Henry—T	2 Nov	at New York Giants	7-7	T	4,000
Rip Kyle—C	7 Nov	at Hartford Blues	7-16	L	4,500
Joe Little Twig—E	11 Nov	at Providence Steamrollers	2-21	L	4,000
Cliff Marker—E	14 Nov	at Brooklyn Lions	0-19	L	7,000
Wade McRoberts—C	21 Nov	Duluth Eskimos	2-10	L	n/a
Don Nelson—T	25 Nov	Akron Indians	0-0	T	n/a
John Nichols—G	28 Nov	at Chicago Bears	0-35	L	5,000
Harry Robb—BB					
Stan Robb—E					
Guy Roberts—WB					
Ben Roderick—WB					
Jack Sack—G					
Frank Seeds—WB					
Dutch Speck—G					
Russ Stein—E					
Jim Thorpe—TB					
Dick Vick—TB					
Dutch Wallace—G					
Harold Zerbe—E					

1926 Columbus Tigers (1-6, 19th)

Head coach—Jack Heldt
Home field—West Side Athletic Club

Roster		Results			
Player—Position	Date	Opponent	Score		Crowd
Pete Barnum—TB	19 Sep	at Chicago Cardinals	0-14	L	2,500
Bill Berrehsem—T	26 Sep	at Canton Bulldogs	14-2	W	2,500
Jim Bertoglio—FB	3 Oct	at Pottsville Maroons	0-3	L	n/a
John Conley—T	10 Oct	at Providence Steamrollers	0-19	L	n/a
Herb Davis—WB	16 Oct	Kansas City Cowboys	0-9	L	5,000
Earl Duvall—T	23 Oct	at Brooklyn Lions	12-20	L	8,000
Flop Gorrill—E	7 Nov	at Buffalo Rangers	0-26	L	3,500
Jack Heldt—G					
Len Johnson—BB					
Joe Mulbarger—G					
Tommy Murphy—BB					
Frank Nesser—G					
Ike Nonenmaker—E					
Harley Pearce—E					
Boni Petcoff—T					
Earl Plank—E					
Bob Rapp—WB					
Lou Reichel—C					
Flash Woods—WB					

1926 Dayton Triangles (1-4-1, 17th)

Head coach—Carl Storck
Home field—Triangle Park

Roster		Results		
Player—Position	Date	Opponent	Score	Crowd
Faye Abbott—FB	3 Oct	at Buffalo Rangers	3-0 W	5,000
Johnnie Becker—T	10 Oct	at Pottsville Maroons	6-24 L	n/a
Art Beckley—BB	17 Oct	Buffalo Rangers	6-7 L	1,500
Jack Brown—G	14 Nov	at Detroit Panthers	0-0 T	n/a
Eric Calhoun—T	20 Nov	at Frankford Yellowjackets	0-35 L	6,000
Dick Dobeleit—WB	21 Nov	at Hartford Blues	0-16 L	n/a
Lee Fenner—E				
Al Graham—G				
Mack Hummon—E				
Hobby Kinderdine—C				
Johnnie Layport—T				
Arnie Mahrt—BB				
Lou Mahrt—TB				
Gene Mayl—E				
Lou Partlow—TB				
Peck Reiter—G				
Ed Sauer—T				

1927 Cleveland Bulldogs (8-4-1, 4th)

Head coach—Roy Andrews
Home field—Luna Park Stadium

Roster		Results		
Player—Position	Date	Opponent	Score	Crowd
Roy Andrews—T	25 Sep	at Green Bay Packers	7-12 L	4,500
Carl Bacchus—E	2 Oct	New York Giants	0-0 T	3,000
Herm Bagby—FB	9 Oct	New York Yankees	7-13 L	n/a
Al Bloodgood—TB	16 Oct	at New York Giants	6-0 W	25,000
Hal Broda—E	23 Oct	at Chicago Bears	12-14 L	n/a
Lester Caywood—T	30 Oct	Duluth Eskimos	21-20 W	12,000
Tom Cobb—T	6 Nov	New York Yankees	15-0 W	2,500
Cookie Cunningham—E	12 Nov	at Frankford Yellowjackets	0-22 L	6,000
Herb DeWitz—BB	13 Nov	Frankford Yellowjackets	37-0 W	5,000
Tiny Feather—FB	20 Nov	at Providence Steamrollers	22-0 W	12,000
Benny Friedman—TB	24 Nov	at New York Yankees	30-19 W	15,000
Dosey Howard—G	27 Nov	at Chicago Cardinals	32-7 W	5,000
Frank Kelley—WB	3 Dec	Duluth Eskimos	20-0 W	11,000
Jerry Krystl—T				
Harry McGee—G				
Lyle Munn—E				
Bill Owen—T				
Gordon Peery—BB				
Proc Randels—E				
Milt Rehnquist—G				
Jim Simmons—WB				
Clyde Smith—C				
Rex Thomas—WB				
Dutch Webber—E				
Ossie Wiberg—BB				
Dick Wolf—WB				

1927 Dayton Triangles (1-6-1, 10th)

Head coach—Lou Mahrt
Home field—Triangle Park

Roster		Results		
Player—Position	Date	Opponent	Score	Crowd
Faye Abbott—TB	18 Sep	at Green Bay Packers	0-14 L	3,600
Sneeze Achiu—WB	24 Sep	at Frankford Yellowjackets	6-3 W	7,000
Johnnie Becker—T	2 Oct	New York Yankees	3-6 L	6,000
Bill Belanich—T	8 Oct	at Frankford Yellowjackets	0-0 T	4,000
Earl Britton—FB	9 Oct	at Chicago Cardinals	0-7 L	2,500
Jack Brown—C	23 Oct	at Providence Steamrollers	0-7 L	6,500
Augie Cabrinha—WB	30 Oct	at Chicago Bears	6-14 L	8,000
Ebby DeWeese—G	13 Nov	at Green Bay Packers	0-6 L	2,500
Lee Fenner—E				
Al Graham—G				
Sam Hipa—E				
Red Joseph—E				
Zip Joseph—E				
Hobby Kinderdine—C				
Lou Mahrt—TB				
Lou Partlow—TB				
Peck Reiter—G				
Ed Seibert—T				
Frank Sillin—WB				
Jimmy Tays—BB				
Corl Zimmerman—G				

COMPLETE STANDINGS

1928 Dayton Triangles (0-7, 10th)

Head coach—Faye Abbott
Home field—Triangle Park

Roster		Results			
Player—Position	Date	Opponent		Score	Crowd
Faye Abbott—BB	29 Sep	at Frankford Yellowjackets		0-6 L	4,000
Sneeze Achiu—WB	7 Oct	at Chicago Cardinals		0-7 L	n/a
Johnnie Becker—T	14 Oct	at Providence Steamrollers		0-28 L	7,000
Bill Belanich—T	20 Oct	at Frankford Yellowjackets		9-13 L	7,000
Earl Britton—FB	28 Oct	at Green Bay Packers		0-17 L	3,100
Jack Brown—C	11 Nov	at Chicago Bears		0-27 L	5,000
Win Charles—TB	29 Nov	at Detroit Wolverines		0-33 L	n/a
Clair Cook—WB					
Ebby DeWeese—BB					
Dick Faust—T					
Al Graham—C					
Clarence Graham—WB					
Sam Hipa—E					
Mack Hummon—E					
Jack Keefer—TB					
Hobby Kinderdine—C					
Carl Mankat—E					
Art Matsu—BB					
Ed Seibert—G					
Frank Sillin—WB					
Jim Spencer—G					
Aubrey Strosnider—T					
Corl Zimmerman—G					

1929 Dayton Triangles (0-6, 12th)

Head coach—Faye Abbott
Home field—Triangle Park

Roster		Results		
Player—Position	Date	Opponent	Score	Crowd
Faye Abbott—FB	22 Sep	at Green Bay Packers	0-9 L	5,000
Johnnie Becker—T	28 Sep	at Frankford Yellowjackets	7-14 L	7,000
Bill Belanich—T	29 Sep	at Providence Steamrollers	0-41 L	8,500
Johnny Brewer—WB	6 Oct	at Staten Island Stapletons	0-12 L	6,000
Jack Brown—C	13 Oct	at Boston Bulldogs	0-41 L	800
Steve Buchanan—TB	24 Nov	at Chicago Cardinals	0-19 L	300
Roy Carlson—E				
John Depner—E				
Pat Duffy—FB				
Dick Faust—T				
Lee Fenner—E				
Al Graham—G				
Bob Haas—BB				
John Kauffman—T				
Hobby Kinderdine—C				
Carl Mankat—T				
Lou Partlow—FB				
Frank Sillin—BB				
John Singleton—TB				
Jim Spencer—G				
Ed Tolley—G				
Tillie Voss—T				
John Wallace—E				
Elmer Wynne—FB				
Corl Zimmerman—G				

1930 Portsmouth Spartans (5-6-3, 8th)

Head coach—Hal Griffen
Home field—Universal Stadium

Roster

Player—Position
Walt Ambrose—G
Chuck Bennett—WB
Chuck Braidwood—E
Richard Brown—C
Koester Christensen—E
Ebby DeWeese—G
Jap Douds—T
Byron Eby—TB
Lee Fenner—E
Bill Fleckenstein—E
Bill Glassgow—TB
Al Graham—C
Aaron Grant—C
Hal Griffen—T
Duke Hanny—T
Dud Harris—T
George Hastings—T
Lou Jennings—E
Spider Johnson—T
Red Joseph—E
Cy Kahl—BB
Tiny Lewis—FB
Father Lumpkin—BB
Babe Lyon—T
Emil Mayer—E
Chief McLain—FB
Ernie Meyer—G
Ray Novotny—TB
Frosty Peters—TB
Carroll Ringwalt—G
Fred Roberts—G
Sod Ryan—T
Ron Schearer—T
Vin Schleusner—T
Gene Smith—C
Buck Weaver—G
Bull Wesley—C

Results

Date	Opponent	Score		Crowd
14 Sep	Newark Tornadoes	13-6	W	4,000
24 Sep	Brooklyn Dodgers	12-0	W	6,000
5 Oct	Chicago Cardinals	0-0	T	6,500
8 Oct	Frankford Yellowjackets	39-7	W	n/a
12 Oct	at Minneapolis Redjackets	0-13	L	2,000
22 Oct	Chicago Bears	7-6	W	7,500
26 Oct	at Chicago Cardinals	13-23	L	8,000
2 Nov	at Green Bay Packers	13-47	L	7,500
5 Nov	New York Giants	6-19	L	7,000
9 Nov	at Staten Island Stapletons	13-13	T	5,000
15 Nov	at Frankford Yellowjackets	6-7	L	3,500
30 Nov	at Chicago Bears	6-14	L	6,000
7 Dec	Minneapolis Redjackets	42-0	W	3,500
14 Dec	Green Bay Packers	6-6	T	4,500

1931 Cleveland Indians (2-8, 8th)

Head coaches—Al Cornsweet, Hoge Workman
Home field—Cleveland Stadium

Roster		Results		
Player—Position	Date	Opponent	Score	Crowd
Chuck Braidwood—E	13 Sep	at Green Bay Packers	0-26 L	5,000
Algy Clark—HB	18 Sep	at Chicago Bears	0-21 L	6,000
Al Cornsweet—FB	26 Sep	Brooklyn Dodgers	6-0 W	2,000
Hank Critchfield—C	7 Oct	at Portsmouth Spartans	0-6 L	n/a
David Cullen—G	18 Oct	at Providence Steamrollers	13-6 W	6,000
Fred Danziger—FB	8 Nov	Chicago Cardinals	6-14 L	10,000
Doc Elliott—FB	15 Nov	at Portsmouth Spartans	6-14 L	4,742
Mike Gregory—G		(at Cincinnati, Ohio)		
Hoot Herrin-C	21 Nov	at Providence Steamrollers	7-13 L	n/a
John Hurley—E	22 Nov	at Staten Island Stapletons	7-16 L	n/a
Merle Hutson—G	28 Nov	at Chicago Cardinals	0-21 L	1,500
Leo Jensvold—HB				
Ernie Jessen—T				
Al Jolley—T				
Red Joseph—E				
Howie Kriss—HB				
Buck Lamme—E				
Biff Lee—G				
Franklin Lewis—FB				
Tiny Lewis—FB				
Babe Lyon—T				
Stu MacMillan—C				
Dave Mishel—TB				
George Munday—T				
Al Nesser—E				
Ray Novotny—HB				
Carl Pignatelli—HB				
Don Ridler—T				
Jim Tarr—E				
Otto Vokaty—FB				
Dale Waters—E				
Chuck Weimer—HB				
Drip Wilson—C				
Hoge Workman—TB				

1931 Portsmouth Spartans (11-3, 2nd)

Head coach—Potsy Clark
Home field—Universal Stadium

Roster			Results		
Player—Position	Date	Opponent	Score		Crowd
Gene Alford—WB	13 Sep	Brooklyn Dodgers	14-0	W	7,000
Bob Armstrong—G	23 Sep	Chicago Cardinals	13-3	W	8,000
Chuck Bennett—WB	30 Sep	New York Giants	14-6	W	10,000
Maury Bodenger—G	7 Oct	Cleveland Indians	6-0	W	n/a
John Cavosie—BB	15 Oct	Frankford Yellowjackets	19-0	W	5,000
George Christensen—T	18 Oct	at Brooklyn Dodgers	19-0	W	10,000
Dutch Clark—TB	25 Oct	at Staten Island Stapletons	20-7	W	12,000
Jap Douds—T	31 Oct	at Frankford Yellowjackets	14-0	W	5,000
Harry Ebding—E	1 Nov	at New York Giants	0-14	L	32,500
Ox Emerson—G	8 Nov	at Chicago Bears	6-9	L	25,000
George Hastings—T	11 Nov	Staten Island Stapletons	14-12	W	n/a
Tony Holm—FB	15 Nov	Cleveland Indians	14-6	W	4,742
Cy Kahl—BB		(at Cincinnati, Ohio)			
Biff Lee—G	22 Nov	at Chicago Cardinals	19-20	L	5,000
Louie Long—E	29 Nov	Chicago Bears	3-0	W	9,000
Father Lumpkin—BB					
Bill McKalip—E					
Chief McLain—FB					
Dutch Miller—C					
Buster Mitchell—E					
Les Peterson—E					
Glenn Presnell—TB					
Clare Randolph—C					
Fred Roberts—G					
Vin Schleusner—T					
Elmer Schwartz—FB					
Deck Shelley—WB					
Stud Stennett—WB					
John Wager—C					
Dale Waters—T					

APPENDIX

1932 Portsmouth Spartans (6-2-4, 3rd)

Head coach—Potsy Clark
Home field—Universal Stadium

Roster		Results		
Player—Position	Date	Opponent	Score	Crowd
Gene Alford—WB	25 Sep	New York Giants	7-0 W	6,000
Bob Armstrong—T	2 Oct	Chicago Cardinals	7-7 T	3,725
Maury Bodenger—G	9 Oct	at Green Bay Packers	10-15 L	5,500
John Cavosie—FB	16 Oct	at Staten Island Stapletons	7-7 T	7,500
George Christensen—T	20 Oct	at Staten Island Stapletons	13-6 W	5,000
Dutch Clark—TB	30 Oct	at New York Giants	6-0 W	n/a
Ray Davis—C	6 Nov	at Brooklyn Dodgers	17-7 W	25,000
Harry Ebding—E	13 Nov	at Chicago Bears	13-13 T	5,500
Ox Emerson—G	20 Nov	Boston Braves	10-0 W	5,000
Hal Griffen—C	27 Nov	Chicago Bears	7-7 T	7,500
Ace Gutowsky—FB	4 Dec	Green Bay Packers	19-0 W	12,000
Father Lumpkin—BB		NFL Playoff Game		
Bill McKalip—E	18 Dec	at Chicago Bears	0-9 L	11,198
Danny McMullen—G		(at Chicago Stadium)		
Buster Mitchell—E				
Glenn Presnell—TB				
Clare Randolph—C				
Am Rascher—T				
Dave Ribble—T				
Fred Roberts—G				
John Wager—G				
Mule Wilson—WB				

1933 Cincinnati Reds (3-6-1, 4th Western)

Head coaches—Al Jolley, Mike Palm
Home field—Redland Field

Roster

Player—Position		Results		
	Date	Opponent	Score	Crowd
Frank Abruzzino—C	17 Sep	at Portsmouth Spartans	0-21 L	5,000
Jim Bausch—TB	8 Oct	Chicago Cardinals	0-3 L	1,500
Mil Berner—C	11 Oct	at Pittsburgh Pirates	3-17 L	5,000
Tom Blondin—G	15 Oct	at Brooklyn Dodgers	0-27 L	12,000
Chuck Braidwood—E	22 Oct	Pittsburgh Pirates	0-0 T	900
Lloyd Burdick—T	5 Nov	Philadelphia Eagles	0-6 L	500
John Burleson—T	12 Nov	at Chicago Cardinals	12-9 W	6,000
Lester Caywood—G	19 Nov	Portsmouth Spartans	10-7 W	7,500
Algy Clark—BB	26 Nov	at Philadelphia Eagles	3-20 L	10,000
Red Corzine—FB	3 Dec	Brooklyn Dodgers	10-0 W	3,500
Joe Crakes—E				
Sonny Doell—T				
Leo Draveling—T				
Chief Elkins—WB				
Rosie Grant—G				
Hal Hilpert—E				
Biff Lee—G				
Gil LeFebrve—TB				
Jim Mooney—E				
Don Moses—BB				
Lee Mulleneaux—FB				
George Munday—T				
Mike Palm—WB				
Lew Pope—TB				
Dick Powell—E				
John Rogers—C				
Kermit Schmidt—E				
Bill Senn—TB				
Seaman Squyres—TB				
Cookie Tackwell—E				
Ossie Wiberg—FB				
Blake Workman—TB				

1933 Portsmouth Spartans (6-5, 2nd Western)

Head coach—Potsy Clark
Home field—Universal Stadium

Roster			Results	
Player—Position	Date	Opponent	Score	Crowd
Gene Alford—WB	17 Sep	Cincinnati Reds	21-0 W	5,000
Maury Bodenger—G	24 Sep	New York Giants	17-7 W	7,000
Ben Boswell—T	1 Oct	Chicago Cardinals	7-6 W	n/a
Jim Bowdoin—G	8 Oct	at Green Bay Packers	0-17 L	5,200
John Burleson—T	15 Oct	at Boston Redskins	13-0 W	21,000
Ernie Caddell—WB	18 Oct	at Philadelphia Eagles	25-0 W	3,500
John Cavoise—FB	5 Nov	at New York Giants	10-13 L	15,000
George Christensen—T	12 Nov	Green Bay Packers	7-0 W	7,500
Ray Davis—G	19 Nov	at Cincinnati Reds	7-10 L	7,500
Red Davis—TB	26 Nov	at Chicago Bears	14-17 L	9,000
Harry Ebding—E	3 Dec	Chicago Bears	7-17 L	10,000
Earl Elser—T				
Ox Emerson—G				
Ace Gutowsky—FB				
Ramey Hunter—E				
Father Lumpkin—BB				
Buster Mitchell—T				
Glenn Presnell—TB				
Clare Randolph—C				
Elmer Schaake—FB				
John Schneller—E				
Harry Thayer—T				
John Wager—G				
Mule Wilson—WB				

1934 Cincinnati Reds (0-8, 6th Western)

Head coach—Algy Clark
Home field—Crosley Field

Roster		Results		
Player—Position	Date	Opponent	Score	Crowd
Gene Alford—WB	9 Sep	at Pittsburgh Pirates	0-13 L	14,164
Gump Arial—E	23 Sep	Chicago Cardinals	0-9 L	6,000
Ed Aspatore—T		(at Dayton, Ohio)		
Tom Bushby—WB	30 Sep	Chicago Bears	3-21 L	5,500
Lester Caywood—G	7 Oct	Chicago Cardinals	0-16 L	2,500
Algy Clark—BB	14 Oct	at Green Bay Packers	0-41 L	3,000
Red Corzine—EB	21 Oct	at Chicago Bears	7-41 L	11,000
Earl Elser—T	28 Oct	Detroit Lions	0-38 L	4,800
Tiny Feather—WB		(at Portsmouth, Ohio)		
Rosie Grant—G	6 Nov*	at Philadelphia Eagles	0-64 L	2,000
Homer Hanson—G				
Foster Howell—T		*Reds folded after Nov. 6 game.		
Russ Lay—G		Franchise moved to St. Louis		
Biff Lee—G		and played last three games there.		
Gil LeFebvre—TB		St. Louis went 1-2.		
Bill Lewis—BB				
Tal Maples—C				
Jim Mooney—E				
Cliff Moore—WB				
Buster Mott—BB				
Lee Mulleneaux—FB				
George Munday—T				
Bill Parriott—FB				
Lew Pope—TB				
Ratterman—HB				
John Rogers—C				
Harvey Sark—G				
Pete Saumer—TB				
Benny Sohn—WB				
Norris Steverson—TB				
Cookie Tackwell—E				
Otto Vokaty—FB				
Cole Wilging—E				
Basil Wilkerson—E				
Charlie Zunker—T				

Notes

Introduction

1. Paul Gallico, *The Golden People* (New York: Doubleday & Company, 1965), 27.
2. David Neft, Richard Cohen, and Rick Korch, *The Football Encyclopedia* (New York: St. Martin's Press, 1994), 19.
3. Gallico, *The Golden People*, 27–28.
4. Neft, Cohen, and Korch, *The Football Encyclopedia*, 19.
5. Neft, Cohen, and Korch, *The Football Encyclopedia*, 19–20.
6. Bob Carroll, Michael Gershman, David Neft, and John Thorn, *Total Football II: The Official Encyclopedia of the National Football League* (New York: HarperCollins Publishers, 1999).

Chapter 1: Lester H. Higgins

1. Canton Public Library; *Akron Beacon Journal*, May 6, 1969, B5; *Canton Repository*, September 17, 1970, 40. Some Higgins quotes were taken from a June 1976 NFL Films interview.
2. *Canton Daily News*, September 18, 1920.
3. Dutch Speck (1886–1952). College: None. Positions: guard, center, tackle. Teams: Canton Bulldogs 1920–1923, 1925–1926; Akron Pros 1924.
4. Jim Thorpe (1887–1953). College: Carlisle Indian School. Positions: tailback, fullback. Teams: Canton Bulldogs 1915–1920, 1926, Cleveland Indians 1921, Oorang Indians 1922–1923, Rock Island Independents 1924–1925, New York Giants 1925, Chicago Cardinals 1928. Thorpe was elected to the Pro Football Hall of Fame in 1963. For more on Thorpe, see Robert W.

Wheeler, *Jim Thorpe: World's Greatest Athlete* (Norman: University of Oklahoma Press, 1975).

5. Joe F. Carr (1879–1939) was a former assistant sports editor of the *Ohio State Journal* and manager of the Columbus Panhandles professional football team before becoming the second president of the NFL in 1921, replacing Jim Thorpe. He stayed in office until his death on May 20, 1939. Carr was elected to the Pro Football Hall of Fame in 1963. For more on Carr, see George Sullivan, *Pro Football's All-Time Greats* (New York: G.P. Putnam's Sons, 1968), 28–31.

6. Al Feeney (1891–1950). College: Notre Dame. Position: center. Team: Canton Bulldogs 1920–1921. Feeney also played for the Fort Wayne (Indiana) Friars in the pre-NFL era.

7. Milt Ghee (1891–1975). College: Dartmouth. Position: tailback. Teams: Chicago Tigers 1920, Cleveland Indians 1921.

8. Guy Chamberlin (1894–1967). College: Nebraska Wesleyan, Nebraska. Position: end. Teams: Decatur Staleys 1920, Chicago Staleys 1921, Canton Bulldogs 1922–1923, Cleveland Bulldogs 1924, Frankford Yellowjackets 1925–1926, Chicago Cardinals 1927. Chamberlin won five NFL titles as a player-coach and was elected to the Pro Football Hall of Fame in 1965. For more on Chamberlin, see Sullivan, *Pro Football's All-Time Greats*, 127–130.

9. Johnny Kyle (1898–1974). College: Indiana. Position: fullback. Team: Cleveland Indians 1923.

Chapter 2: Joseph F. Carr

1. None of the six Nesser brothers attended college; they all worked in the Panhandle Division of the Pennsylvania Railroad. Al Nesser (1893–1967) played guard, end; Frank Nesser (1889–1953) played fullback, tackle, guard; Fred Nesser (1887–1967) played tackle, end, fullback; John Nesser (1876–?) played guard, tackle; Phil Nesser (1880–1959) played guard, tackle, wingback; Ted Nesser (1883–1941) played center, tackle, guard. The six Nesser siblings hold the NFL record for most brothers from one family who have played in the NFL. They also hold the distinction of having the only father-son combination to ever play together. Charles Nesser played with his father Ted in several NFL games during the 1921 season.

2. The office building at 16 East Broad Street in Columbus, Ohio, was the headquarters of the NFL from 1927 until 1939. *Columbus City Directories, 1927–1939.*

3. Johnny Unitas (1933–2002). College: Louisville. Position: quarterback. Teams: Baltimore Colts 1956–1972, San Diego Chargers 1973. Unitas was elected to the Pro Football Hall of Fame in 1979.

4. Red Grange (1903–1990). College: Illinois. Position: halfback. Teams: Chicago Bears 1925, 1929–1934; New York Yankees (AFL) 1926; New York Yankees (NFL) 1927. Grange was an All-American halfback at Illinois and

became the biggest name in football when he scored four touchdowns in the first twelve minutes against powerhouse Michigan in 1924. After his senior year in college in 1925, he decided to turn pro. Because there wasn't a college draft, Grange was free to sign with whichever team he wanted. So he signed to play for the Chicago Bears. Five days after his last college game, Grange and the Bears played seventeen games in three months on two different barnstorming tours. Because of Grange's turning pro, the NFL took a big hit from the public for raiding colleges and universities for its players. Because of Grange, the NFL established a rule in 1926 prohibiting college players from playing professional football until after their college class had graduated. The NFL called it the "Grange Rule." For more on Grange, see John M. Carroll, *Red Grange and the Rise of Modern Football* (Urbana: University of Illinois Press, 1999).

5. The Green Bay Packers were found guilty of using college-eligible players during the 1921 NFL season. J. E. Clair forfeited the franchise during the NFL meeting on January 28, 1922. Later, in the spring, Curly Lambeau paid the fifty-dollar fine and promised to never break the rule again. The Packers were able to rejoin the NFL.

6. Former NFL owners George Halas of the Chicago Bears, Art Rooney of the Pittsburgh Steelers, Tim Mara of the New York Giants, and George Preston Marshall of the Washington Redskins are all enshrined in the Pro Football Hall of Fame.

7. Joe Carr died on May 20, 1939, from a second heart attack. *Ohio State Journal,* May 21, 1939.

8. Ray Didinger, "The Man Who Had a Dream," *Pro!* (New York: National Football League Properties, 1977, Volume 7, Issue 5), C14.

Chapter 3: Fritz Pollard

1. John M. Carroll, *Fritz Pollard: Pioneer in Racial Advancement* (Urbana: University of Illinois Press, 1992).

2. Clair Purdy (1895–1950). College: Brown. Position: wingback. Teams: Rochester Jeffersons 1920, New York Brickley's Giants 1921, Milwaukee Badgers 1922. Purdy played for the Akron Pros in 1919 as a teammate of Fritz Pollard.

3. Frank Neid (1894–1955) was the co-owner of the Akron Pros football team with Art Ranney. Neid was the owner of the Hamilton Cigar Store on Mill Street in Akron. Neid was nicknamed the "Mayor of Mill Street." Art Ranney (1889–1970) was an engineer for Summit County. During the NFL's organizational gathering in Canton on September 17, 1920, it was Ranney who kept the league minutes; those meeting minutes have been preserved by the Pro Football Hall of Fame.

4. Pete Calac (1892–1968). College: Carlise Indian School, West Virginia Wesleyan. Positions: fullback, wingback. Teams: Canton Bulldogs 1920,

1925–1926, Cleveland Indians 1921, Washington Senators 1921, Oorang Indians 1922–1923, Buffalo Bisons 1924.
5. Paul Robeson (1898–1976). College: Rutgers. Positions: end, tackle. Teams: Akron Pros 1921, Milwaukee Badgers 1922. Robeson went on to have a career in the movie and music industries. For more on Robeson, see Martin Bauml Duberman, *Paul Robeson* (New York: Alfred A. Knopf, 1989).
6. Joe Guyon (1892–1971). College: Carlise Indian School, Georgia Tech. Positions: fullback, wingback. Teams: Canton Bulldogs 1920, Cleveland Indians 1921, Washington Senators 1921, Oorang Indians 1922–1923, Rock Island Independents 1924, Kansas City Cowboys 1925, New York Giants 1927. Guyon was elected to the Pro Football Hall of Fame in 1966. For more on Guyon, see Sullivan, *Pro Football's All-Time Greats*, 164–166.
7. National Football League, *2003 National Football League Record & Fact Book* (New York: National Football League Properties, 2003), 395.

Chapter 4: Nesser Brothers

1. Newspaper headlines read by interviewee from Keith McClellan, *The Sunday Game: At the Dawn of Professional Football* (Akron: University of Akron Press, 1998), 49–63.
2. *Columbus Dispatch*, January 27, 2002. Knute Rockne gained fame as the head coach of the University of Notre Dame, but before his coaching career, Rockne played professional football in South Bend and for the Massillon Tigers.
3. Two younger Nessers played football for Ohio State University. William H. Nesser lettered for the Buckeyes in 1928–1929; William F. Nesser lettered in 1947–1949.

Chapter 5: George "Hobby" Kinderdine

1. Harry "Shine" Kinderdine (1893–1947). College: None. Position: guard. Team: Dayton Triangles 1924. Walt Kinderdine (1899–1964). College: None. Positions: fullback, tailback. Team: Dayton Triangles 1923–1925.
2. Sneeze Achiu (1902–1989). College: Dayton, Hawaii. Positions: wingback, tailback. Team: Dayton Triangles 1927–1928.
3. On Sunday October 3, 1920, the first two games in NFL history—APFA in 1920—involving two league teams took place: the Dayton Triangles against the Columbus Panhandles, and the Muncie Flyers against the Rock Island Independents. Because the Triangles-Panhandles game was played in the eastern time zone, it has been credited with being the first-ever NFL game. Dayton won 14-0, while Rock Island defeated Muncie 45-0.
4. Si Burick was a sportswriter for the *Dayton Daily News*. Burick was inducted into the writer's wing of the Baseball Hall of Fame in 1986.

5. Russ Hathaway (1896–1988). College: Indiana. Positions: tackle, guard. Teams: Muncie Flyers 1920, Dayton Triangles 1920–1924, Canton Bulldogs 1922, Pottsville Maroons 1925–1926, Buffalo Bisons 1927.

Chapter 6: Lee Fenner

1. Al Mahrt (1893–1970). College: Dayton. Positions: tailback, wingback. Team: Dayton Triangles 1920–1922.
2. *Dayton Daily News,* September 26, 1927.
3. In 1930, John Dwyer, a Brooklyn businessman, purchased the Dayton Triangles. He moved the team to New York and renamed them the Brooklyn Dodgers.
4. Steve Presar runs a website about the Dayton Triangles at www.daytontriangles .org.

Chapter 7: Ike Roy Martin

1. The Fort Wayne (Indiana) Friars were a professional football team in the pre-NFL days. Several of their players came and played in Ohio during the early years of the NFL. For more on the Friars, see McClellan, *The Sunday Game,* 38–48, 324–345.
2. Howard "Cap" Edwards (1888–1944). College: Notre Dame. Position: guard. Teams: Canton Bulldogs 1920–1921, Toledo Maroons 1922, Cleveland Indians 1923, Cleveland Bulldogs 1924.
3. In 1920 the Canton Bulldogs finished in third place in the NFL with a 7-4-2 record.
4. Bob "Nasty" Nash (1892–1977). College: Cornell, Rutgers. Positions: tackle, end. Teams: Akron Pros 1920, Buffalo All-Americans 1921–1923, Rochester Jeffersons 1924, New York Giants 1925.

Chapter 8: Arda Bowser

1. Bowser played for the Frankford Yellowjackets in 1922 as well as the Canton Bulldogs. The Yellowjackets were a professional team but not a member of the NFL until 1924.
2. The Oorang Indians were an NFL franchise for two seasons in 1922–1923. They were formed by Walter Lingo, a dog kennel owner, who wanted to advertise his business. He got together with his good friend Jim Thorpe and formed a pro football team made up of Native Americans entirely. During their two years in the NFL, they compiled a record of 4-16. The team disbanded after the 1923 season. For more on the Oorang Indians, see Robert L.

Whitman, *Jim Thorpe and the Oorang Indians* (Defiance: The Marion County Historical Society, 1984).
3. In the 1912 Olympic Games, Jim Thorpe won gold medals in the decathlon and pentathlon. He was declared the "Greatest Athlete in the World" by King Gustav V of Sweden. But later it was revealed that Thorpe played professional baseball in North Carolina for fifteen dollars a game and was declared ineligible. His two medals were taken away. In January of 1983, the United States Olympic Committee finally restored Thorpe's amateur status and returned his two medals to the Thorpe family.
4. Nick "Long Time Sleep" Lassa (1898–1964). College: Carlise Indian School, Haskell Indian School. Positions: tackle, end, center. Team: Oorang Indians 1922–1923. Duke Osborn (1897–1976). College: Penn State. Positions: guard, center. Teams: Canton Bulldogs 1921–1923, Cleveland Bulldogs 1924, Pottsville Maroons 1925–1928.
5. Cecil "Tex" Grigg (1891–1968). College: Austin, Texas. Positions: tailback, wingback. Teams: Canton Bulldogs 1920–1923, Rochester Jeffersons 1924–1925, New York Giants 1926, Frankford Yellowjackets 1926.
6. Wallace "Doc" Elliott (1900–1976). College: Lafayette. Positions: fullback, tailback. Teams: Canton Bulldogs 1922–1923, Cleveland Bulldogs 1924–1925, Cleveland Indians 1931.

Chapter 9: Art Haley

1. Bruce "Scotty" Bierce (1896–1982). College: Akron. Position: end. Teams: Akron Pros 1920–1922, 1925; Cleveland Indians 1923; Buffalo All-Americans 1923; Cleveland Bulldogs 1924.
2. *Canton Repository*, October 11, 1920.

Chapter 10: Walter Lingo

1. The Oorang Airedale was a new type of dog developed by Walter Lingo. The Airedale was groomed for hunting and sporting purposes. For more on the Oorang Airedale, see Bryan D. Cummings, *Airedales: The Oorang Story* (Calgary, Alberta: Detseling Enterprises Ltd., 2001).
2. Paul Brown (1908–1991). College: Miami of Ohio; Coach: Cleveland Browns 1946–1962; Owner: Cincinnati Bengals 1968–1991. Brown was elected to the Pro Football Hall of Fame in 1967.
3. Whitman, *Jim Thorpe and the Oorang Indians*, 81.

Chapter 11: William Guthery, Sr.

1. Many celebrities, such as Lou Gehrig, Charley Paddock, Ty Cobb, and Jack Dempsey, bought Oorang Airedales from Walter Lingo.

2. Lo Boutwell (1892–1969). College: Carlise Indian School. Positions: wing-back, fullback. Team: Oorang Indians 1922–1923.

Chapter 12: William Roy "Link" Lyman

1. The 1922 Canton Bulldogs won the NFL championship with a 10-0-2 record.
2. After the 1923 season, Cleveland Indians owner Sam Deutsch bought the financially struggling Canton Bulldogs and moved the team to Cleveland. He renamed the team the Cleveland Bulldogs. The Bulldogs went on to win the NFL championship with a 7-1-1 record. The following spring, he sold the Canton franchise back to Canton and the Cleveland franchise to a new local owner, Herbert Brandt.
3. Wilbur Pete "Fats" Henry (1897–1952). College: Washington & Jefferson. Position: tackle. Teams: Canton Bulldogs 1920–1923, 1925–1926; New York Giants 1927; Pottsville Maroons 1927–1928. Henry was elected to the Pro Football Hall of Fame in 1963.
4. In December of 1959, Canton sportswriter Chuck Such challenged the city of Canton to make the town the site of the Pro Football Hall of Fame. By February of 1962, the city raised over $370,000 and had a site picked out. The owners approved the site, and on August 11, 1962, the city broke ground to build the shrine. In 1963, the first class of seventeen charter members was inducted. For more on the history of the Pro Football Hall of Fame, see Mike Rathet and Don Smith, *Their Deeds and Dogged Faith* (New York: Balsam Press, 1984).
5. Link Lyman gave his Hall of Fame speech in Canton, Ohio, on September 6, 1964.

Chapter 13: Hal Broda

1. Benny Friedman (1905–1982). College: Michigan. Positions: quarterback, tailback, defensive back. Teams: Cleveland Bulldogs 1927, Detroit Wolverines 1928, New York Giants 1929–1931, Brooklyn Dodgers 1932–1934. The 1927 Cleveland Bulldogs finished in fourth place in the NFL with an 8-4-1 record. They led the NFL in scoring with 209 points.
2. The Providence Steamrollers played their NFL home games at the Cyclodrome from 1925–1931.
3. Dan Daly and Bob O'Donnell, *The Pro Football Chronicle* (New York: Macmillan Press, 1990), 40.

Chapter 14: Glenn Presnell

1. Ed Weir (1903–1991). College: Nebraska. Positions: tackle, end. Team: Frankford Yellowjackets 1926–1928. Ken Strong (1906–1979). College: New

York University. Positions: fullback, tailback. Teams: Staten Island Stapletons 1929–1932; New York Giants 1933–1935, 1939, 1944–1947. Strong was elected to the Pro Football Hall of Fame in 1967. For more on Strong, see Sullivan, *Pro Football's All-Time Greats*, 213–217.

2. Nick McMahon was the manager of the semipro Ironton Tanks team in Ironton, Ohio. He signed Glenn Presnell to a pro contract in 1928.

3. Earle "Greasy" Neale (1891–1973). College: West Virginia Wesleyan; played for several professional teams in the pre-NFL days, including the Dayton Triangles and the Ironton Tanks. Neale became a head coach later, coaching the Philadelphia Eagles from 1941–1950 and winning NFL championships in 1948 and 1949. Neale was elected to the Pro Football Hall of Fame in 1969. For more on Neale, see Bob Curran, *Pro Football's Rag Days* (New York: Prentice Hall, Inc., 1969), 33–46. Willis Glassgow (1907–1959). College: Nebraska, Iowa. Position: tailback. Teams: Portsmouth Spartans 1930, Chicago Cardinals 1931. Chief McLain (1905–1983). College: Haskell Indian School, Iowa. Position: fullback, halfback. Teams: Portsmouth Spartans 1930–1931, Staten Island Stapletons 1931. Chuck Bennett (1907–1973). College: Indiana. Position: wingback. Teams: Portsmouth Spartans 1930–1931, Chicago Cardinals 1933.

4. Gene Alford (1905–1975). College: Sul Ross State, Texas Tech. Positions: wingback, defensive back. Teams: Portsmouth Spartans 1931–1933, Cincinnati Reds 1934, St. Louis Gunners 1934.

5. The Portsmouth Spartans were an NFL franchise for four years (1930–1933) until they were sold to G. A. Richards, a radio man, who moved the team to Detroit and renamed it the Detroit Lions. For more on the Portsmouth Spartans, see Carl M. Becker, *Home & Away: The Rise and Fall of Professional Football on the Banks of the Ohio, 1919–1934* (Athens: Ohio University Press, 1998).

6. Potsy Clark (1894–1972). College: William & Vashti, Illinois. Head coach: Portsmouth Spartans 1931–1933; Detroit Lions 1934–1936, 1940; Brooklyn Dodgers 1937–1940. Clark won an NFL championship with the Lions in 1935.

7. Earl "Dutch" Clark (1906–1978). College: Colorado College. Positions: tailback, defensive back. Teams: Portsmouth Spartans 1931–1932, Detroit Lions 1934–1938. Clark was also the head coach for the Detroit Lions in 1937–1938 and the Cleveland Rams in 1939–1942. Clark was elected to the Pro Football Hall of Fame in 1963. For more on Clark, see Curran, *Pro Football's Rag Days*, 89–96.

8. Roy "Father" Lumpkin (1907–1974). College: Georgia Tech. Positions: fullback, linebacker. Teams: Portsmouth Spartans 1930–1933, Detroit Lions 1934, Brooklyn Dodgers 1935–1937.

9. In 1932 the Chicago Bears (6-1-6) and the Portsmouth Spartans (6-1-4) were tied for first place in the NFL standings. After the season finale, the league office arranged for an additional regular-season game to determine the league champion. The game was moved indoors to Chicago Stadium because of a heavy snowstorm. The field was only 80 yards long, and the sidelines came right up to the wall. The goal posts were moved from the end lines to the goal lines, and for safety, inbounds lines or hash marks were used for the first time,

which meant moving the ball in 10 yards away from the wall. On December 18, the Bears won 9-0, scoring the only touchdown on a 2-yard pass from Bronko Nagurski to Red Grange. The Spartans protested the pass, claiming Nagurski wasn't 5 yards behind the line of scrimmage when he threw the ball, which was the rule at that time. Because of this game, the following spring at the league meetings, several new rules were adopted: hash marks were established for the first time; goal posts were moved to the front of the end zone to encourage more field goals; and passing became legal from anywhere behind the line of scrimmage, which opened up the passing game. Also the owners agreed on splitting the league into two divisions and having the two winners meet in a championship game, similar to baseball's World Series.

10. Bronko Nagurski (1908–1990). College: Minnesota. Positions: fullback, linebacker, tackle. Team: Chicago Bears 1930–1937, 1943. Nagurski was elected to the Pro Football Hall of Fame in 1963. For more on Nagurski, see Jim Dent, *Monster of the Midway: Bronko Nagurski, the 1943 Chicago Bears, and the Greatest Comeback Ever* (New York: Thomas Dunne Books, St. Martin's Press, 2003).

11. George A. Richards bought the Portsmouth Spartans in the spring of 1934. He moved the franchise to Detroit and renamed them the Lions.

12. On December 15, 1935, the Detroit Lions defeated the New York Giants 26-7 at the University of Detroit football field; 15,000 fans attended.

Chapter 15: Dr. Louis Chaboudy

1. The Portsmouth Spartans finished their four years in Portsmouth with records of 5-6-3 in 1930, 11-3-0 in 1931, 6-2-4 in 1932, and 6-5 in 1933.

2. Ernie Caddell (1911–1992). College: Stanford. Positions: wingback, defensive back. Teams: Portsmouth Spartans 1933, Detroit Lions 1934–1938. Ox Emerson (1907–1998). College: Texas. Positions: guard, linebacker. Teams: Portsmouth Spartans 1931–1933, Detroit Lions 1934–1937, Brooklyn Dodgers 1938.

3. For more on the 1931 Packers-Spartans "Iron Man Game," see Becker, *Home & Away*, 281–284.

4. John "Shipwreck" Kelly (1910–1986). College: Kentucky. Positions: tailback, defensive back. Teams: New York Giants 1932; Brooklyn Dodgers 1933–1934, 1937. Cal Hubbard (1900–1977). College: Centenary, Geneva. Positions: tackle, guard. Teams: New York Giants 1927–1928, 1936; Green Bay Packers 1929–1933, 1935; Pittsburgh Pirates 1936. Hubbard was elected to the Pro Football Hall of Fame in 1963 and was elected to the Baseball Hall of Fame in 1976 as an umpire. He is the only man enshrined in both Halls of Fame. For more on Hubbard, see Sullivan, *Pro Football's All-Time Greats,* 55–58. Johnny "Blood" McNally (1903–1985). College: Wisconsin-River Falls, St. John's (Minnesota), Notre Dame. Positions: halfback, wingback, defensive back. Teams: Milwaukee Badgers

1925; Duluth Eskimos 1926–1927; Pottsville Maroons 1928; Green Bay Packers 1929–1933, 1935–1936; Pittsburgh Pirates 1934, 1937–1938. McNally was also head coach for the Pittsburgh Pirates 1937–1939. McNally was elected to the Pro Football Hall of Fame in 1963. For more on McNally, see Myron Cope, *The Game That Was* (New York: Thomas Y. Crowell Company, 1970), 46–56.

5. Cyrus Kahl (1904–1971). College: North Dakota. Positions: fullback, wingback. Team: Portsmouth Spartans 1930–1931.

6. George Christensen (1909–1968). College: Oregon. Positions: tackle, guard. Teams: Portsmouth Spartans 1931–1933, Detroit Lions 1934–1938.

7. The town of Portsmouth held a reunion for the old Spartans players on August 4, 1970. To honor the former NFL team, the town renamed the old stadium where they played from Universal Stadium to Spartan Stadium.

8. Becker, *Home & Away*, 222.

Chapter 16: Leo Blackburn

1. Jim Thorpe played for the 1927 Portsmouth Shoe-Steels, a semipro team in Portsmouth, Ohio. For more on Thorpe's playing for the Shoe-Steels, see Becker, *Home & Away*, 148–157.

2. Ernie Nevers (1903–1976). College: Stanford. Position: fullback. Teams: Duluth Eskimos 1926–1927, Chicago Cardinals 1929–1931. Nevers was elected to the Pro Football Hall of Fame in 1963. For more on Nevers, see Jim Scott, *Ernie Nevers, Football Hero* (Minneapolis: T. S. Denison & Company, 1969).

3. The Portsmouth Spartans lost to the Cincinnati Reds 10-7 on November 19, 1933. The Reds were 1-5-1, and the Spartans were 6-2 at the time of the game. The loss knocked the Spartans out of the Western Division race.

4. Bill Kuenzel of the *Detroit News* snapped a famous photo of Dutch Clark that first appeared in the paper. Later it was featured in a 1937 issue of *Life* magazine.

5. Leo Blackburn himself gave a copy of his "Super Bowl Reflections" to the author on July 1, 2000.

Chapter 17: Earl "Dutch" Clark

1. Alan Gould was an Associated Press writer from Pittsburgh who placed Clark on his first-team All-American squad in 1929.

2. During 1934–1935 the city of Detroit saw the following events: the Detroit Tigers defeated the Chicago Cubs four games to two, winning the World Series; the Detroit Redwings lost the Stanley Cup finals three games to one to the Chicago Blackhawks; the Detroit Lions defeated the New York Giants 26-7 to win the NFL championship.

3. Ted Marchibroda (1931–). College: St. Bonaventure, Detroit Mercy. Position: quarterback. Teams: Pittsburgh Steelers 1953, 1955–1956; Chicago Cardinals 1957.
4. Sullivan, *Pro Football's All-Time Greats*, 34.
5. Arthur Daley, *Pro Football's Hall of Fame*, (New York: Grosset & Dunlap, 1963), 140.

Chapter 18: Cyrus Kahl

1. Undated poem from the *Portsmouth Times*. From the author's collection.

Chapter 19: Norris Steverson

1. Cecil Mulleneaux (1908–1985). College: Northern Arizona. Positions: center, linebacker, wingback. Teams: New York Giants 1932, Cincinnati Reds 1934, St. Louis Gunners 1934, Pittsburgh Pirates 1935–1936, Chicago Cardinals 1938, Green Bay Packers 1938.
2. The Cincinnati Reds joined the NFL in 1933. Poor attendance and poor play on the field hurt the franchise. Although a second season was attempted in 1934, the team disbanded midway through the season after compiling a record of 0-8. The St. Louis Gunners, an independent pro team, was granted permission to take over the Reds' remaining schedule and finished with a record of 1-2.

Appendix

1. Bob Carroll, Michael Gershman, David Neft, John Thorn, *Total Football II: The Official Encyclopedia of the National Football League* (New York: HarperCollins Publishers, 1999*)*.
2. Bob Gill and Tod Maher, *The Pro Football Encyclopedia* (New York: MacMillan Company, 1997).
3. National Football League, *2004 National Football League Record & Fact Book* (New York: National Football League Properties, 2004).

Index

Achiu, Sneeze, 26
Agajanian, Ben, 24
Akron, Ohio, xiv, 14–15, 17, 44,
    46–47, 63, 69, 99
Akron Beacon-Journal, 1
Akron Pros, xiv, 12, 15, 17, 27, 34,
    44–46, 63
Alexandria, Minnesota, 92
Alford, Gene, 69
American Professional Football Asso-
    ciation, ix, 1–2, 5, 7, 17, 27–28, 32
Anderson, Gary, 24
Arizona State University, 95–98
Aurora, Ohio, 35

Baltimore Colts, 8
Beaver Falls, Pennsylvania, 44–45
Bennett, Chuck, 69
Benson, Kate, 18
Bethany College, 37
Bierce, Bruce, 44–45
Blackburn, Leo, 81–85
Blackburn, Tom, 81–82
Blanda, George, 24
Boutwell, Lo, 55
Bow, Clara, 96
Bowser, Arda, 36–43

Broda, Hal, 62–66
Brooklyn, New York, 30
Brooklyn Dodgers, 80
Brown, Paul, 51
Brown University, 12, 14–15, 62, 64,
    66
Buck, Cub, 34
Bucknell University, 36–39
Buffalo, New York, 34
Buffalo All-Americans, 56
Burick, Si, 27

Caddell, Ernie, 77
Calac, Pete, 15, 34, 41, 48, 55, 59,
    63
Calhan, Colorado, 68
Camp, Walter, 12, 14
Canton, Ohio, xi, xiv, 1–4, 15, 32,
    38–41, 44, 58–59, 62–63, 65–66, 99
Canton Bulldogs, xii–xiv, 1–4, 15, 29,
    32, 34, 36, 38, 43–46, 57–59,
    62–63
Canton Citizens Savings Bank, 2
Canton Daily News, 1
Canton McKinley High School, 62
Canton Public Library, 1
Canton Repository, 1

Carillon Historical Park, 30
Carlisle Institute, 50
Carr, Dennis, 10–11
Carr, Gregory, 10–11
Carr, James, 5–11
Carr, John, 10
Carr, Joseph, Jr., 6
Carr, Joseph F., xiv, 5–11, 19–20, 22, 31, 58–59, 72, 78
Carr, Mary, 6
Carr, Michael, 10–11
Carr, Velda, 11
Carroll, Bird, 59
Case (Western Reserve) University, 45, 62, 64–65
Cassady, Irene, 18
Centerville, Ohio, 27
Chaboudy, Louis, 75–80
Chamberlin, Guy, 4, 58–59, 61, 63
Chicago, Illinois, 2–3, 8, 12–13, 29, 41–42, 57, 59, 65, 72, 79
Chicago Bears, 9, 41, 57, 59, 70–72, 74, 77, 79, 82, 86, 89, 95, 97
Chicago Cardinals, 42, 65, 83
Chicago Stadium, 72, 79
Christensen, George, 79, 82, 90
Cincinnati, Ohio, xiv, 69–70, 75, 83, 99
Cincinnati Reds, 83, 95, 97–99
Clark, Earl "Dutch," 71–72, 77, 82–83, 86–91
Clark, Potsy, 70–71, 73, 78–79, 86, 88, 90–91
Cleveland, Ohio, xiv, 4, 43, 66, 99
Cleveland Browns, 74
Cleveland Bulldogs, xiv, 57, 59, 62, 65–66
Cleveland Indians, 4, 36, 40, 43
Cleveland Rams, 86, 90, 99
College Football Hall of Fame, 12
Colorado College, 72, 82, 86–88
Colorado School of Mines, 86, 89
Columbus, Ohio, xiv, 5–11, 19–20, 22–23, 48, 69, 99
Columbus Dispatch, 78
Columbus Panhandles, 5, 7, 10, 18–23, 26, 46, 55

Comstock, Rudy, 59
Coon Pawn Inn, 55
Cornell University, 28
Costas, Joe, 39
Creighton University, 68
Cubs Park, 30
Cusack, Jack, 2
Cuyahoga Falls High School, 44–45
Cyclodrome, 65

Danville, Pennsylvania, 36
Dartmouth College, 13–14, 27
Dayton, Ohio, xiv, 25–27, 28–31, 44, 99
Dayton Daily News, 30
Dayton Gym-Cadets, 26, 29
Dayton Triangles, 25–27, 28–31, 44, 46
Dayton University, 81–82
Delaware, Ohio, 52
Dempsey, Jack, xi, 54
Denver College, 88
Detroit, Michigan, 70–71, 73, 75, 78, 83, 86–87, 89–90
Detroit Free Press, 21
Detroit Lions, 67, 73–74, 79, 83, 86, 89–90
Detroit News, 90
Detroit Tigers, 89
Deutsch, Jordan A., xii
Deutsch, Sam, 59
DeWitt, Nebraska, 68
Dooley, John, 38
Dorais, Gus, 34
Driscoll, Paddy, 61
Duluth Kelleys, 24

East Tech High School, 66
Eastern Kentucky University, 67
Edwards, Cap, 34
Elliott, Doc, 42–43, 58
Emerson, Ox, 71, 77, 79, 84

Feeney, Al, 3, 34
Fenner, Lee, 28–31
Fenner, Mark, 28, 31
Fort Pierce, Florida, 56

Fort Wayne, Indiana, 32–33
Fort Wayne Friars, 32–34
Fort Wayne Journal-Gazette, 21
Fowler, Colorado, 86–87
Franco–Prussian War, 18
Frankford Athletic Association, 64
Frankford Yellowjackets, 30, 38, 42, 57, 62, 64
Friedman, Benny, 65–66, 78
Fritz Pollard Alliance, 16

Gallico, Paul, xi–xii
Gehrig, Lou, xi, 54
General Motors, 25–28
Georgia Tech University, 76
German Village, 20
Germany, 18
Ghee, Milt, 3
Gilberton, Pennsylvania, 16
Gilead, Nebraska, 67–68
Glassgow, Willis, 69
Glenville High School, 66
Gould, Alan, 88
Graham, Theresa, 18
Grange, Harold "Red," xi, 8, 16, 30, 59, 61, 65, 68, 70, 72, 78, 82, 95, 97
Green Bay Packers, 8, 71, 74, 77–78, 83–85
Griggs, Cecil, 41, 58
Guthery, William, Sr., 53–56
Guyon, Joe, 15, 34, 41, 48, 50, 53, 59–60, 63

Halas, George, 9, 41, 51, 58–59, 61, 71–72, 95, 97
Haley, Art, 44–46
Hammond, Indiana, 3, 16
Hammond Pros, 12
Hanson, Jason, 74
Harding, Warren G., xi
Harrisburg, Pennsylvania, 39
Hathaway, Russ, 27
Hay, Lulu, 1–2
Hay, Ralph, 1–4, 39, 41–42, 58
Healey, Ed, 60–61
Heaton, North Dakota, 92
Heidelberg College, 33

Henderson, L. T., 76
Henry, Pete "Fats," 1, 58–59, 61, 63
Heslop, Ann, 44–46
Heslop, Donald, 46
Heslop, Tim, 45–46
Hewitt, Bill, 61
Higgins, Lester H., 1–4
Hopkins, Ted, 18–19
Horween, Ralph, 42
Hubbard, Cal, 78
Hyde Park, Illinois, 13

Indianapolis, Indiana, 55
Ironton, Ohio, 67, 69–70, 73–74
Ironton Tanks, 67, 69–70, 77

J. P. Loomis Company, 46
James, Frank, 32
Jones, Ben, 59
Jones, Bobby, xi

Kahl, Alma, 92–94
Kahl, Cyrus, 79, 92–94
Kansas City Cowboys, 69
Kellogg, Steve, 61
Kelly, John "Shipwreck," 78
Kiesling, Walt, 61
Kinderdine, George, 25–27
Kinderdine, Harry, 25–26
Kinderdine, Jack, 25–26
Kinderdine, James, 26
Kinderdine, Jim, 25, 27
Kinderdine, Virginia, 25–27
Kinderdine, Walt, 25–26
Kohler Manufacturing, 2
Kuenzel, Bill, 90
Kyle, Johnny, 4

Lafayette College, 37
Lakeside Park, xii
Lakeview High School, 13
Lane Tech, 13–14
LaRue, Ohio, xiv, 48–50, 52–56, 99
LaRue High School, 53–54
LaRue News, 55
Lassa, Nick "Long Time Sleep," 41, 55–56

League Park, 43
Lewisburg, Pennsylvania, 38–40
Liberty, Missouri, 32
Liberty High School, 33
Life, 83, 90
Lingo, Bob, 48–52
Lingo, Walter, 48–54
Lock, Gordon, 64
Lumpkin, Father, 71, 76–77, 79, 82, 84, 94
Lyman, William Roy "Link," 57–61, 63

Mahrt, Al, 29
Mara, Tim, 9
Marchibroda, Ted, 90
Marino, Dan, 66
Marion, Ohio, 54–55
Marshall, Bobby, 24
Marshall, George Preston, 9
Martin, Ike Roy, 32–35
Massillon, Ohio, 3
Massillon Independent, 21
Massillon Tigers, 3, 18, 62
McCreary, Aaron, 97
McLain, Chief, 69
McMahon, Nick, 69
McNally, Johnny "Blood," 78
Mechanicsburg, Ohio, 55
Mesa, Arizona, 95, 98
Miami Dolphins, 24
Miamisburg, Ohio, 25, 27
Miamisburg High School, 25
Middlebranch, Ohio, 1–2
Miller Brewing Company, 31
Milwaukee Badgers, 12, 16
Mt. Carmel, Indiana, 39
Mulleneaux, Cecil, 97
Murdick, Terri, 18
Musso, George, 61

Nagurski, Bronko, 61, 72, 74, 82, 91, 95, 97
Nash, Bob "Nasty," 34
National Football League, xi, xiv, 1, 5–11, 16–18, 22, 25–31, 35–36, 42–43, 45, 47–48, 51–52, 56, 58–59, 61, 69–71, 73, 76, 78, 85, 89, 91, 95, 97, 99
Neale, Earle "Greasy," 69–70
Neid, Frank, 14
Nesser, Al, 18–19, 46
Nesser, Charlie, 18
Nesser, Frank, 18–19
Nesser, Fred, 18–19
Nesser, John, 18–19, 23
Nesser, Katherine, 18–19
Nesser, Pete, 19
Nesser, Phil, 18–19
Nesser, Ray, 18–20
Nesser, Rose, 19–20
Nesser, Ted, 18–19, 21
Nesser, Theodore, 18–19
Nesser Brothers, 7, 10, 18–23, 46
Nesser Family Reunion, 10, 18
Nevers, Ernie, 83
New Bloomington, Ohio, 55
New Rochelle, New York, 12
New York, New York, 8–9, 29, 65
New York Daily News, xii
New York Giants, 9, 47, 69, 72–73, 77, 89
New York University, 68
New York Yankees, 30, 65
Newton, Kansas, 87
NFL Films, 12, 32, 36, 42
North Dakota University, 92–94
Northwestern University, 87
Notre Dame University, 3, 32, 34, 58, 90

O'Donnell, Pepper, 34
Oakland Raiders, 24
Oberlin College, 45
Ohio River, 75
Ohio State Journal, 5, 7
Ohio State University, 10, 22
Olympic Medals, 41
Oorang Bang, 56
Oorang Dog Kennels, 48, 55
Oorang Indians, 40–41, 48–52, 53–56
Osborn, Duke, 41, 58, 63

Paddock, Charley, 54
Pasadena Rose Parade, 60
Penn State University, 15
Pennsylvania Railroad, 7, 19–20
Philadelphia, Pennsylvania, 38–39, 42
Pittsburgh, Pennsylvania, 36–37, 75
Pittsburgh (Pirates) Steelers, 9, 73
Pittsburgh Plate and Glass Company, 46
Plain Dealer (Cleveland), 55
Pollard, Fritz, 3, 12–16, 63, 66
Pollard, Hughes, 13
Pollard, Luther, 13
Polo Grounds, 30
Portsmouth, Ohio, xiv, 70–71, 73, 75–80, 81–85, 92–94, 99
Portsmouth Spartans, 28, 30, 67, 69–74, 75–80, 81–85, 86, 88–89, 92–94
Portsmouth Times, 80–81
Portsmouth Universal Stadium, 80
Presar, Steve, 30
Presnell, Glenn, 67–74, 75, 77–79, 82, 84
Presnell, Mary, 73
Pro Football Hall of Fame, xiv, 5–6, 10–11, 16, 18, 23, 57, 59–60, 68–69, 73, 75, 77–79, 82, 86–87, 91
Providence Steamrollers, 12, 16, 65, 69
Purdy, Clair, 14

Recreation Field, 20
Reynolds, Pete, 37–38
Richards, George A., 67, 73, 78, 86, 89
Rickey, Branch, 11
Ripley's Believe It or Not, 41
Robb, Harry, 58
Robeson, Paul, 15
Robinson, Jackie, 11
Rockne, Knute, 18, 21, 34
Rogers Park, Illinois, 12–13
Rooney, Art, 9
Rose Bowl, 12, 14

Russell, Kentucky, 70
Rutgers University, 15
Ruth, Babe, xii

San Diego Chargers, 24
Schneider, John, 18–19, 22
Seattle Bombers, 90
Secrist, Jim, 79
Sefton, Fred, 45
Shawnee State University, 84
Shelby Shoe Company, 75, 83
Sherman, Babe, 18
Silver Springs, Maryland, 16
Smyth, Louie, 58
Snyder, Harry, 71–73
Spartan Stadium, 75, 79, 94
Speck, Dutch, 2, 34, 58
St. Joseph, Missouri, 34
St. Louis Cardinals, 11
St. Louis Gunners, 97
Stanford University, 77
Steverson, Margaret, 98
Steverson, Norris, 95–98
Stivers High School (Dayton), 28
Storck, Carl, 31
Strong, Ken, 68, 78
Syracuse University, 38

Table Rock, Nebraska, 57–58
Tampa Bay Buccaneers, 98
Tennessee Titans, 24
Thorpe, Jim, 2–3, 7, 15, 26, 29, 32, 34, 40–41, 44–46, 48–50, 52–56, 58–60, 62–63, 82
Thousand Oaks, California, 79
Tilden, Bill, xi
Tobin, Elgie, 12, 14
Toledo, Ohio, xiv, 99
Trafton, George, 60–61
Triangle Park, 27, 29–30
Tulsa Oilers, 95, 98
Turner, Charles, 21

Umstattd, William, 60
Unitas, Johnny, 8
University of Akron, 44–45

University of Arizona, 96–97
University of California–Berkley, 61
University of Dayton, 26
University of Detroit, 90
University of Indiana, 69
University of Iowa, 69
University of Kentucky, 27
University of Minnesota, 92
University of Nebraska, 57–58, 61, 67–68

Washington & Jefferson College, 1
Washington Redskins, 9, 99
Washington State University, 12, 14
Weir, Ed, 68
Weissmuller, Johnny, xi

West Carrollton, Ohio, 25
West Virginia University, 73, 93
William Jewell College, 32–34
Wills, Helen, xi
Wilmington College, 81–82
Winter Park, Florida, 36, 42
Wolf Creek, 29
Wooster College, 45
World War I, xi, 15, 36
World War II, 99
Wrigley Field, 30, 72

Yorkville, Indiana, 27
Young, Steve, 66

Zanesville, Ohio, 46

About the Author

Chris Willis has worked in the Archives Department at NFL Films as head of the Research Library since 1996. As the resident historian at NFL Films, he oversees all aspects of research for the company and their producers. In 2002 he was nominated for an Emmy for his work on the HBO documentary "The Game of Their Lives: Pro Football in the 1950s." He is also a member of the College Football Historical Society (CFHS) and the Professional Football Researchers Association (PFRA). Several of his articles, including "The Pro Football Hall of Fame—The Beginning," "The Bodyguard and Johnny U," "Ralph Hay: Forgotten Pioneer," and "Joe Carr's Vision," have been published in the PFRA publication *The Coffin Corner*.

In 1997 and 1998, he gave oral presentations at the Pro Football and American Life Symposiums held at the Pro Football Hall of Fame. Before starting at NFL Films, he graduated with a B.S. in physical education from Urbana (Ohio) University—while playing four years on the Urbana football team—and attended one year of graduate school at Ohio State University in sports history. Willis is a native of Columbus, Ohio, and currently resides in Moorestown, New Jersey.